New Guinea: the tide is stemmed

D1592611

New Guinea:
the tide is stemmed
John Vader

Editor-in-Chief: Barrie Pitt
Editor: David Mason
Art Director: Sarah Kingham
Picture Editor: Robert Hunt
Designer: David A Evans
Cover: Denis Piper
Special Drawings: John Batchelor
Photographic Research: John Moore/Benedict Shephard
Cartographer: Richard Natkiel

Photographs for this book were especially selected from the following Archives: from left to right pages 4-5 Australian War Memorial; 7 Australian War Memorial; 8-9 National Archives; 10 Imperial War Museum; 11-15 National Archives; 20 Australian War Memorial; 21 Keystone; 23 Keystone; 24 Bell Aircraft Corporation/Australian War Memorial; 25 Australian War Memorial/IWM; 28-29 National Archives; 30 Australian War Memorial; 32-33 IWM; 34 National Archives/US Navy; 35 IWM; 36 National Archives; 38 Australian War Memorial; 39 National Archives; 40-41 US Air Force; 42 National Archives; 44 National Archives; 45 IWM/National Archives; 46 US Army/US Air Force; 47-49 Australian War Memorial; 52 Australian War Memorial; 53 US Army; 54-56 Australian War Memorial; 59 US Air Force; 61-72 Australian War Memorial; 74 US Army/Australian War Memorial; 75 IWM; 76 US Army; 80-86 Australian War Memorial; 87 US Army; 88 Australian War Memorial; 89 US Army; 91-99 Australian War Memorial; 100 IWM; 104-111 Australian War Memorial; 112 US Army; 113 Australian War Memorial; 116 US Army; 117-122 Australian War Memorial; 122-123 US Air Force; 123 Australian War Memorial; 125 IWM; 128 US Army; 129-130 Australian War Memorial; 131 US Army; 132 Australian War Memorial; 133 US Army; 134-136 Australian War Memorial; 136 US Army/IWM; 139-143 US Army; 144 National Archives; 145 Australian War Memorial; 146 National Archives; 150 US Marine Corps; 151 National Archives; 155-158 Australian War Memorial
Front Cover: Australian War Memorial
Back Cover: Australian War Memorial

First Printing: April 1971
Printed in United States of America

Ballantine Books Inc.
101 Fifth Avenue New York NY 10003

An Intext Publisher

Contents

The writing on the wall

Introduction by Barrie Pitt

The Japanese success at Pearl Harbor was the detonator which initiated their explosive expansion through the Western Pacific and Southeast Asia. At one point on the fringe of the blast lay New Guinea – and the valuable base of Port Moresby. To secure their frontier in this direction it was vital to the invaders that this key area be taken and held. Unfortunately for them Australians chose to contest the point.

Before the outbreak of hostilities in the Pacific, Australian opinion on the likelihood of Japan becoming involved in a world war, despite the warnings of the military pundits, who had been predicting a 'yellow peril' invasion for forty years, mirrored that widespread in the western world. A sanguine view was prevalent, based on a complete misconception of the state of Japan's preparedness. In particular the ridiculous though comfortable belief that Japanese industry produced nothing but inferior copies of western machines enjoyed great favour; this notwithstanding the chilling evidence from the Chinese theatre. The real state of affairs of course was that the Japanese possessed a modern navy larger than the US Pacific Fleet, a superior air force of brilliantly flown bombers and fighters – including the unparalleled Zero, and an efficient, thoroughly trained army. The numbing shock of disillusion when the disciplined, well equipped hordes swept all before them in an oriental Blitzkrieg awoke the continent from dream to nightmare reality.

Understandably, many Australians feared that their country would be next on the list. As it happened Japan had no immediate plans for invasion, but raids on the mainland could easily be viewed as the beginning of a preliminary softening up operation; and nothing seemed beyond the inflamed ambition of the triumphant conquerors. New Guinea and the Port Moresby strongpoint were seen as the last bastion of defence.

To the Japanese it was to have been almost a routine operation. Had they not defeated thousands of Allied troops in Malaya, the Philippines and the Netherlands East Indies? New Guinea should have been easy.

Several factors conspired to make it the reverse of easy. There were the difficulties of the overland route across the Owen Stanley Range, the only practical approach to Port Moresby. For most of its length, originally a one man wide trail, it successively burrowed through steaming jungle, scaled mountains and dived into ravines. Maintaining supplies over such a road presents problems. Then the appalling climate which, among other trials, often turned the track into a muddy torrent and caused rapid deterioration of equipment. Thirdly the climate's associated pests, parasites and diseases which weakened and debilitated, turning fit fighting men into

shaky shadows in a few days. And lastly, and by no means least though the foregoing distressful circumstances naturally worked equally adversely on them, the Australians' dogged persistence and courage in resolutely denying the Japanese advance, and more, pushing them back. It must be remembered too that in the vital early stages the Australians were largely untried troops fighting against the experienced and confident victors of a dozen campaigns, and it was not until later that they were joined by veterans from the Near East war and substantial American forces.

Throughout the New Guinea campaign the Allied forces were under the ultimate command of General Douglas MacArthur – and thereby hangs a tale. John Vader's very frank account points up vividly the dangers of misunderstandings and conflicts between command and the troops in the field. MacArthur, impatient and apparently quite without understanding of the unique features of the battleground and the nature of the war being fought there, persistently pressed for spectacular, energetic advances. In his view the troops and their officers were hanging back, not displaying the conspicuous aggressiveness he demanded, and he made no bones about saying so. In fact, in what was for much of the time a guerilla war, the men were fighting – in the worst conditions that could be imagined – intelligently, economically and with supreme bravery. They could have been forgiven if they had shown deep resentment at what could not but be interpreted as repeated slurs on their courage.

However, their magnificent spirit and laconic humour survived more bitter crises than the petty annoyance of ill-informed criticism. They went on to provide the first heartening proof that the enemy could be held and successfully forced backward. What this meant to morale in Burma and the other areas was out of all proportion to the events' strategic significance, and it sent a premonitionary shiver of apprehension through the ranks of the Japanese armed forces.

The struggle for New Guinea began with one naval battle – in the Coral Sea – and Japan's chances finally ended with another – in the Bismarck Sea. The intervening two years were a picture-in-little of the course of the war at large. In the beginning the Allies were weak and almost defenceless against a thoroughly prepared adversary. Grimly they fought back while building up their numbers and weapon strength, and at last were able to mount large frontal attacks on the enemy's base positions. Though the issues were at times being decided by mere handfuls of men compared with the confrontation of hundreds of thousands elsewhere, there was in no theatre more selfless dedication shown, or more praise deserved.

Japan goes to war

When war came to Australia's doorstep in December 1941, her military pundits were not surprised; they had been predicting a 'yellow peril' invasion across the Pacific for forty years. The average Australian however, though not entirely unsuspecting, had been led to believe that a militarily weak (as they thought) Japan would not become involved in a world war. They were shocked, amazed and somewhat apprehensive when Japanese airmen swamped the bulk of the US Pacific Fleet at Pearl Harbor. A few short weeks later transports landed tough, ruthless soldiers on the islands north of the Australian continent.

A new enemy had entered the war and suddenly he was not the ill-equipped, weak-eyed, amateur little soldier Australians had thought him to be; he was a determined, capable, brave, disciplined, well-equipped and ably-led fighter supported, to everybody's surprise, not by tinny warships and antique aircraft, but by a modern navy larger than America's Pacific fleet, and by a superior air force of brilliantly flown bombers and fighters. The shock of the Japanese advance produced a numbness felt by civilians and servicemen throughout the country.

General Karl von Clausewitz (the Liddell-Hart of the 19th century), a Prussian officer present throughout

Napoleon's Russian campaign, said that the object of war was either to overthrow the enemy and dictate terms, or to make some conquests on the frontier of the enemy's country and retain them or use them for exchange in the settlement of peace. Obviously the Japanese war planners waged war for the second objective. But had they followed Clausewitz more closely they would have paid more attention to the delicate situation which arises from that objective. 'The conqueror in a war,' said the Prussian, 'is not always in a position to subdue his adversary completely. Often, in fact almost universally, there is a culminating point of

The Japanese attack Pearl Harbor.
Left: Arizona, Tennessee, **and** *West Virginia* **after the strike.** *Above:* **The destroyer** *Shaw* **explodes**

victory . . . It is necessary to know how far preponderance will reach, in order not to go beyond that point and, instead of fresh advantage, reap disaster . . . to overstep the point at which the offensive changes into the defensive is more than simply a useless expenditure of power yielding no further results, it is a destructive step which causes reaction, and the reaction is, according to all experience, productive of most disproportionate effects.'

Left: The Japanese invade Malaya: a search is carried out on a captured British defender. *Above:* The Sino Japanese war: General Tsai, commanding Nineteenth Army, visits a howitzer position. *Below:* Japanese sailors prepare for an attack

The delicate situation in Japan's thrust was the occupation of New Guinea and their leaders could not believe that having defeated tens of thousands of Allied troops in Malaya, the Philippines and the Netherlands East Indies, they could be held by Australian troops and pushed back along a thin little jungle trail across the Owen Stanley Range at a time when Japan was numerically superior.

This extraordinary battle for New Guinea was a two-year campaign, beginning with guerilla skirmishes fought by untried men against Japan's experienced troops who were supported by superior naval and air forces, and ending when the Allies were able to mount large frontal attacks on the enemy's strong base positions. It was a local example of the course of the larger war, the Allies weak and almost defenceless at first, then fighting back while they slowly built up their numbers and weapon strength. It began with one naval battle – in the Coral Sea – and Japan's chances finally ended with another – in the Bismarck Sea. In the period between these two actions at sea the Japanese attempted to capture their last Pacific objective, Port Moresby, by sending an army overland; they were checked, held and gradually forced back across disease-filled, jungle-clad mountains. In a flanking movement at Milne Bay they were decisively beaten and forced to retreat. The New Guinea campaign was the Australians' war until, towards the end, they fought side by side with their American allies.

The Japanese excuse for imperialist expansion was the enlargement of their 'Co-Prosperity Sphere', an ideal for a new order in the East; they originally called it the 'New Order' but felt that the name had become unpopular by the Nazis' use of it and expected that the term 'Co-Prosperity'

Below: **A Japanese light naval gun during the Sino Japanese conflict.**
Right: **The New Guinea invasion begins**

would appeal more to the peoples of South-East Asia. It was, anyway, only a gimmick; the natives of Japan's oldest colonial possessions – Korea and Formosa – had been exploited for years and had never received any benefits from the phony co-prosperity. And no-one else was clamouring for the Japanese to bring them wealth; instead they were wishing that Japan had not been forced by Admiral Peary, in 1854, to open her ports and re-establish contact with the world. Before the Allies attempted to reverse the Peary effect, Japan had been short of foreign exchange which she tried to rectify by selling cheap goods to a world recovering from a depression – goods which the world was eager to buy and which established too readily the belief that all Japanese products were cheap and unreliable. If the Co-Prosperity Sphere could be established with the Japanese as the ruling race, they felt, possibly quite correctly, that the economies of their subjects would improve. Like the Germans, the Japanese had a great talent for organization, and both races accepted discipline as being part of Nature.

Apart from wanting to break the blockade of oil and other raw materials imposed by Britain, America and Holland, and the desire to forcibly expand into the 'Southern Region', the East Asian Federation Movement (*Toa Renmei Undo*) had promulgated doctrines of domination and expansion since the movement was formed by Major-General Kanji Ishihara in Manchuria during 1931. His plan was for the domination of Manchuria and China only, and by enforcing 'Federation' on Manchuria the result was the China Incident, a war Japan could have lost simply because of the Allies' blockade. Colonel Masanobu wrote: 'The umbilical cord of the Chunking regime runs to England and America. If this is not speedily cut the Sino-Japanese war will drag on endlessly.' However, the Japanese War Party had long had designs on the wealthy countries of the south-west Pacific, and agents of the Party began their surveys years before war was declared. To them, China's wealth was its vast man-power; the Indies, Malaya, the Philippines and Borneo had wealth underground and growing from the soil. Hoping, and no doubt praying, that Germany would win, the Japanese Warriors decided to risk everything and make the big grab: they would send their troops, experienced from fighting in China, into the lands of everlasting summer, and expel the 300,000 whites who were 'oppressing' 100,000,000 natives who, they also hoped and no doubt prayed, would give them enormous strength through coalition.

They made their preparations carefully. The army planning staff lived for almost a year in primitive tropical conditions where they evolved tactics and tested armament and equipment; the result was a planning study of great originality and thoroughness. For the common soldier they printed pamphlets explaining what the war was all about – the various stages, voyages, landings, action, survival and hygiene. The question. 'Why must we fight?' was cynically answered, 'Obeying the Emperor's august will for peace in the Far East'. Malaria, it was stressed, was the Great Enemy: 'To fall in a hail of bullets is to meet a hero's death, but there is no glory in dying of disease or accident through inattention to hygiene or careless-ness . . . in all tropical campaigns since ancient times far more have died through disease than have been killed in battle'. They were taught to wear a cloth under their helmets to absorb sweat and stop it running into their eyes; also to avoid glare and keep the sun as much as possible behind them; to remember that bullets travelled further in heated air; to outflank the enemy at every possible opportunity; to control water points and disinfect them with chloride of lime; to eat boiled, pure rice and salted plums and add salt to their tea. Dried and tinned foods would be issued and the jungle planners found that a preservative tablet would protect boiled rice which each man would carry as his main ration (and somehow they discovered that it was dangerous to drink milk or spirits when eating mangoes); and that just one case of malaria in a group was a dangerous source of infection for them all as the disease could be quickly transmitted by mosquitoes. The little details, from bicycles for Malaya to tablets for the rice, were easily attended to, and the tactics were sound. The grand strategy was the most vital and sensitive part of the overall plan.

Briefly, it was this: the planners called for a simultaneous attack on Pearl Harbor, Malaya and the Philippines, then an advance into the Netherlands East Indies, occupation of Burma and finally securing the 'Southern Region' with a strong defensive perimeter running from the Indian border, through Burma, Malaya, Sumatra, Java, Timor, New Guinea, the Bismarck Archipelago, the Mar-

shall and Gilbert Islands, across Wake Island and ending at the Kuriles. Australia would be left out on a limb, isolated by Japanese warships and air forces from any immediate worthwhile aid from America.

The Japanese accomplished what they set out to do, practically on schedule, except that they were frustrated in their plan to take Port Moresby, and frustrated by US Marines who were to go on the offensive in the Solomons, the large collection of islands east of the captured Archipelago. Interlacing the islands with lines of invasion, threading down between Indo-China and the Philippines, Borneo and Malaya, Sumatra and Java, Borneo and the Celebes, attacking the main Allied bases with only a quarter of their Army strength, the Japanese – in a hundred days – destroyed Allied power in the Far East. Another quarter of the enemy's

Captured Japanese rations, including a supply of whisky

forces was readied for an onslaught on Russia from Siberia; the other half was engaged in China. After another hundred days the enemy generals and admirals, if they could allow themselves to be honest, would see that victory for them was not at all possible unless Germany could help them out, and by then Germany was already contained.

The Japanese were over-confident. Their Twenty-fifth Army advanced 600 miles and conquered Malaya in seventy days, a feat unparalleled in military history. Singapore, with no rear defences, fell to a blitzkrieg on bicycles. The Japanese High Command attributed success to the patriotic fervour of front-line officers and men, and again were over-confident, believing that these officers and men would never cease to sweep all before them. The New Guinea Campaign developed as a result of the Japanese leaders' persistent determination to capture one little port; an ingrained determination that became a mania as the project increasingly changed from a logical strategic move to a gamble.

The Allied embargo on oil, iron and steel against Japan was also observed by Australia. In 1938 the Prime Minister, Robert Menzies, had sanctioned some exports of scrap metal to the Japanese and was dubbed by the waterside workers 'Pig-iron Bob'. Ever since Japan defeated Russia in the 1904–5 war Australians were wary of any military growth in Japan or China. That war had changed the anti-militaristic attitude of the people, who remained, however, emphatic that they would not be part of any imperialistic adventure in which Britain might become involved. Compulsory military training for home defence was accepted and a militia was established; but should Australia ever become involved in a war overseas, service would be on a voluntary basis only – a parliamentary promise which was not broken until Australians were unwillingly committed to the war in Vietnam.

In those early days of 'to arm or not to arm' a Sydney literary, satirist weekly, *The Bulletin*, was a persistent advocate of vigilance against dangers which could come from Asia. In 1917, one of the journal's contributors, C J Dennis, wrote a prophetic verse regarding his country's trade with Japan; it was called *The Glugs of Gosh* – the story of a people who worked all day for the sake of Slosh and suffered the cant and humbug that communities usually endure from their politicians. The baddies were the Ogs, the people of Podge and, in his story, Dennis warned of buying baubles from Podge (Japan) and selling back the raw materials of munitions. The Glugs traded stones for eight-day clocks, sewing machines, mangles, scissors and sox, and sure enough one day the stones came hurtling back. It was fortunate for the Glugs that eight-day clocks, sewing machines, etc. could also be hurled.

Japan was an ally of Britain during the First War, when Australians experienced their first big test in battle. They had fought well, if undramatically, in the Boer War, and were satisfied with what they achieved in the First World War – at Gallipoli, in Sinai and in the trenches of France. They had rushed to join up in 1914 and rushed again, although not in such numbers, in 1939. An AIF division, the 6th – continuing numerically from the first war AIF – was trained and ready in Palestine when Italy turned North Africa into a battlefield by declaring war in June 1940.

At home, Australia's defence situation was drastically altered when British and French armies were defeated in June 1940. At that time, an Anglo-Australian approach was made to America requesting US naval support for Singapore and for further pressure to be brought against Japan: the Americans replied that they had already fully committed the navy to their own defences. Two months later Churchill cabled that if Japan attempted to invade Australia or New Zealand,

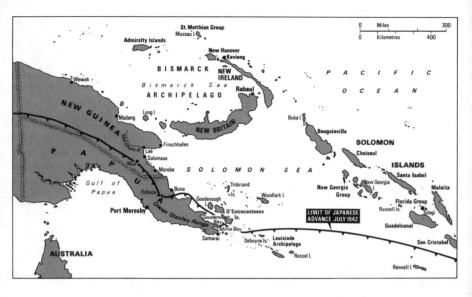

Britain would cut her losses in the Middle East and order out to the Dominions the Mediterranean fleet and all other forces not vital to her own defence and sustenance. As a result of this message a second Australian division, the 7th, was confidently sent to the Middle East and, when representatives of Australia, Burma, India and New Zealand conferred in Singapore, with an American observer attending, a decision was made to strengthen Malaya. Further troops, including the AIF 8th Division, were sent there, and the air force was strengthened. Meanwhile the 6th Division had gone into action in the Desert and a few weeks later part of the 7th and the incomplete 9th had begun their long and glorious stand at Tobruk.

Prime Minister Menzies was beginning to think that Australia had placed too much faith in Britain and was worried that the British government was too unconcerned about Singapore. In fact, the British Chiefs of Staff were

By July 1942 the Japanese had over-reached themselves.

very concerned. Several Japanese militarists admired Churchill's leadership and character which they believed 'savoured of Zen mysticism'. Menzies would not have agreed, for he was forced to report to the Australian War Cabinet that 'Mr Churchill had no conception of the British Dominions as separate entities and the more distant the problem from the heart of the Empire the less he thought about it'. That was in the middle of 1941 when the US government brought Douglas MacArthur out of retirement to command all American army forces in the Far East, and when Japanese assets in the US, Britain and Holland were frozen. The uncertainty of the war situation and Menzies' waning popularity brought a change of government in October that year, and John Curtin, leader of the Labour Party, became the new Prime Minister.

Having opposed conscription for

19

With Australian troops committed in the Middle East home defences were thin

home service two years before, Curtin now had to increase it and make other unpopular decisions about home defence. It was obvious that Australia could be invaded almost anywhere around its long coastline, so the main areas to be defended, apart from places like Port Darwin in the north, were the industrial regions of the south-east, which extended from Newcastle, 100 miles north of Sydney, to Port Kembla, 150 miles south. It was obviously impossible for a few militia divisions and a small air force, even if reinforced a hundredfold, to protectively cover the whole continent, so it was planned to let the north go in the event of an invasion; the Tropic of

Blamey, MacArthur and Prime Minister Curtin meet in Australia to discuss the defence

Capricorn, just north of Brisbane, would be the approximate eastern defence line, the 'Brisbane Line.' Drovers, the 'overlanders', would move cattle down from the north, and country people would be brought into the cities, it was supposed. The Japanese successes were to change all these plans and the war would be tentatively fought wherever the enemy could be held, the further away from Australia the better. The Allies were not to know that Japan had no immediate designs on Australia.

Coral Sea and New Guinea

The air raid that was no drill at Pearl Harbor sank or damaged battleships, cruisers and destroyers. These were not, however, to be the vital naval weapons of the Pacific war; those would be aircraft carriers, and when Nagumo's air fleet attacked there were none in port. *USS Lexington*, based there, was on a plane-ferrying mission to Midway – a duty which contributed to the important battle which was to take place near that island in June, and a duty which undoubtedly preserved the carrier to make an important – but for her, fatal – contribution to the Battle of the Coral Sea. In this oceanic war a carrier would be worth ten battleships; in Europe, where air superiority was all-important, the air forces had airfields, whereas in the Pacific the Allies had carrier decks, and the side which survived with more decks could destroy the opposing air power.

On 7th December, Australia and New Zealand were in a desperate position. Practically all their trained sailors, soldiers and airmen were overseas; there were few aircraft and no capital ships in a position to prevent a determined attack by the enemy. The Australian government urgently sought help from Britain, expecting an immediate, beneficial reaction from the 'mother country' in whose defence Australians (and New Zealanders) had already made sacrifices at sea, on land and in the air; contributions as fine as any made by members of the Commonwealth who had come to her aid. A British division would probably have done as well in the first Desert campaign when Italy temporarily lost Libya – and over 100,000 troops – but it happened to have been won by the Australian 6th Division, supported by British tanks and guns; and that division had fought in Greece and Crete, the 9th had held Tobruk, and the 7th and a brigade of the 6th helped destroy the Vichy army in Syria.

Australia expected a reciprocal effort from Britain, but the difficulties were too great, the distances too immense, the supplies too few and the strategic need, it seemed, too unimportant. Churchill declared war

General Tojo, Japan's War Minister

against Japan before Roosevelt did; Roosevelt decided to ask Congress to declare war on Japan but not Germany. Then, by declaring war on America, on 11th December, Hitler pleased Churchill immensely. Later, he recalled, 'I thought of a remark which Edward Grey had made to me more than thirty years before – that the United States is like "a gigantic boiler. Once the fire is lighted under it, there is no limit to the power it can generate". Being saturated and satiated with emotion and sensation, I went to bed and slept the sleep of the saved and thankful.' In Tokyo, General Tojo should never have had another sound sleep, for he had entered an all-out war with a limited purpose, and the prospect of victory depended a lot on wishful thinking.

Australia turned to America. The common enemy was poised, threatening both countries and particularly the islands – from the Philippines down to New Guinea – that such a short while before were thought to be a barrier. Their common interests coincided. The War Cabinet believed that after the East Indies, Australia would logically be the next objective; the US urgently wanted Australia as a supply base for American forces in the Philippines. And so, within two weeks of war being declared, Washington and Canberra reached an agreement for mutual aid; 4,500 men – few of them combat troops – were on their way to land on 22nd December. An infantry division, the 41st, was sent out in February and by the end of May 36,000 support troops followed. They would all have been too late if the Japanese had maintained their momentum southwards; too late, anyway, to have stopped a landing in northern Australia. Should that have happened, all aid might have been diverted to New Zealand. As the invasion did not eventuate, Australia and New Zealand became firm partners with the US and they all agreed to the establishment of an Anzac Area under an American Supreme Commander. General MacArthur, commanding a last-ditch stand at Bataan, was ordered to escape and, by PT boat and Flying Fortress, brought his staff, wife and son to Darwin where, on 17th March, he made his famous prophesy: '. . . I have come out, and I shall return.' He was received with great ceremony; he was an heroic figure come to help Australians hold back the enemy. However when the AIF 8th Division's commander, General Gordon Bennett escaped without being ordered to do so, at the time that the Singapore GOC decided to surrender, fleeing simply to bring back his detailed knowledge of what happened there, he was virtually snubbed for his trouble; he should have stayed with his troops, rebuked stern, influential generals and politicians at home.

The first incident of real danger to Australia occurred on 23rd January, when the garrison of 1,400 Australians at Rabaul was overcome by a Japanese force of 5,300. Kavieng, in New Ireland, and the rest of New Britain were occupied in the enemy's advance by a flood of troops that seemed inexhaust-

Above: US aircraft refuel in Australia; part of the American aid against the Japanese. *Below:* Joint US-Australian Army manoeuvres in Queensland, Australia

Above: Major-General Gordon Bennett at a press conference in Malaya. *Below:* Major-General L V Bond and Major-General Bennett review reinforcements

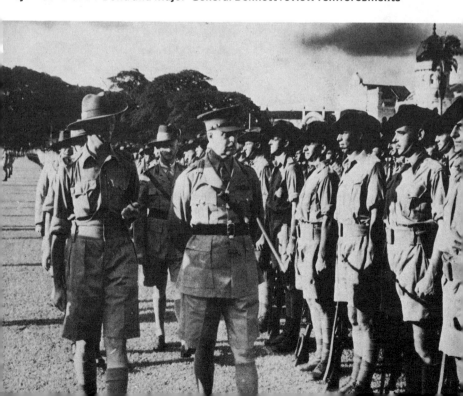

The Consolidated PB Catalina can justly claim to have been the most successful flying boat design of all time. Designed before the war, it exceeded its specifications as a patrol aircraft so handsomely that it was redesignated a patrol-bomber (PB) and went into large scale production for the US Navy. The Catalina served throughout the war in many roles – rescue, patrol/bombing, supply, communication, transport and evacuation. The variant illustrated is a PBY-5A amphibian. *Engines :* Two Pratt & Whitney R-1830 Twin Wasps, 1,200 hp each. *Crew :* 7-9. *Maximum speed :* 179 mph at 7,000 feet. *Cruising speed :* 117 mph. *Ceiling :* 14,700 feet. *Range :* 2,545 miles. *Armament :* Three .3-inch and two .5-inch machine guns plus up to 4,000 lbs of bombs, four 650 pound depth charges or two torpedoes. *Weights empty/loaded :* 20,910/35,420 pounds. *Span :* 104 feet. *Length :* 63 feet 10½ inches

The Commonwealth Aircraft Wirraway was in production for the RAAF at the time of Japan's entry into the war and was quickly pressed into service as an interim fighter in the desperate days of 1942. The type was originally the North American NA-33 trainer, which was selected as Commonwealth Aircraft's first venture into production as it possessed many of the latest innovations in aircraft design, but was not too sophisticated. Before being phased out of front line service in favour of more modern machines, the Wirraway made a great contribution to the stemming of the Japanese advance. *Engine :* Pratt & Whitney S1H1-G Wasp radial, 600hp at 7,000 feet. *Armament :* two fixed and one flexible .303-inch Vickers machine guns and up to 500 pounds of bombs. *Speed :* 205mph. *Climb rate :* 1,950 feet per minute at sea level. *Ceiling :* 23,000 feet. *Range :* 720 miles. *Weight empty/loaded :* 3,980/6,353 lbs. *Span :* 43 feet. *Length :* 27 feet 10 inches

The Commonwealth Aircraft CA-12 Boomerang was designed hurriedly in Australia, after it had been realised that the fighter aircraft available in the theatre were entirely inadequate, and that no supplies of more modern types would be forthcoming from Great Britain and the United States. The design used as many components as possible of the Wirraway trainer in production in Australia and the most powerful engine available in any numbers in the area. The type was too slow to meet Japanese fighters on equal terms, but it proved very rugged and manoeuvrable. It did sterling work in the ground support role. *Engine:* Pratt & Whitney R-1830 radial, 1,200hp. *Armament:* two 20mm Hispano cannon, four .303-inch Browning machine guns and one 500 lbs bomb. *Speed:* 296mph at 7,600 feet. *Climb rate:* 2,490 feet per minute at sea level. *Ceiling:* 34,000 feet. *Range:* 930 miles (on internal fuel). *Weight empty/loaded:* 5,373/8,249 lbs. *Span:* 36 feet. *Length:* 26 feet 9 inches

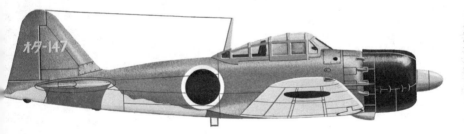

The Mitsubishi A6M Zero came as a complete surprise to the Allies. Convinced that Japanese aircraft were no more than inferior copies of their western counterparts, they were suddenly faced with a superlative fighter aircraft – fast, agile, with a high rate of climb, a good range and a heavy armament. And so at the beginning of the Pacific and South East Asian campaigns the Zero was the prime factor in the skies, and can be said to have had a major influence on Japanese strategic thinking as a result. The type did have two drawbacks, however, and Allied pilots soon learnt to exploit these and so hold the Zeros. These two faults were inadequate protection for pilot and fuel, and a relatively light construction, which meant that the Zero could not take much damage. *Engine:* Nakajima Sakae 21 radial, 1,130 hp. *Armament:* Two 20mm cannon and two 7.7mm machine guns plus up to 264 pounds of bombs. *Maximum speed:* 351 mph at 19,685 feet. *Climb rate:* 4,500 feet per minute. *Ceiling:* 35,100 feet. *Range:* 1,000 miles. *Weight loaded:* 6,047 pounds. *Span:* 36 feet 1 inch. *Length:* 29 feet 8¾ inches

ible, who had reached out thousands of miles from their home islands, their ships and aircraft sinking Allied warships and shooting down almost every Allied plane in the process. With such speed of expansion it was easy enough for them, protected all the way by cruisers and destroyers and without much fear of interception, to land on undefended or partly defended islands. The second incident appeared at first to be a greater danger and was certainly more dramatic: Darwin, a naval and air base on Australia's north-west coast, was bombed on 19th February.

Nagumo, the Japanese admiral who led the attack on Pearl Harbor with his aircraft-carriers *Akagi*, *Hiryu*, *Kaga* and *Soryu*, moved the same task force to the Banda Sea near Timor and launched his attack on a clear, sunny morning. His aircrews were the élite of his country's air forces, their dive-bombing and high-level bombing being more accurate than any Allied air force at that time. The Royal Australian Air Force aircraft stationed at Darwin comprised eleven manned Hudson bombers and fourteen Wirraway single-engined trainers. By sheer chance there were ten USAAF P-40s also at the base where they had stopped on their way to the wasteful vacuum of Java. In the harbour were the US destroyer *Peary*, US seaplane tender *William B Preston*, two sloops and five corvettes of the Royal Australian Navy, and thirty-eight other naval and merchant vessels, the largest being the 12,000-ton transport, *Meigs*. Also, there were two USN Catalina flying boats and a Qantas four-engined flying boat.

When the bombers and Zero fighters flew in, there were five P-40s patrolling in the air while the Squadron's commander, Major Pell, had landed the other five to refuel; they scrambled to join the others and were shot down while taking off. Four of the patrolling P-40s were also shot down while one escaped into cloud after getting two Zeros. This opposition hardly affected the determined flight of the enemy as their aircraft bombed and strafed across the harbour and town. The *Meigs* and seven other merchantmen were sunk or beached, the RAN hospital ship *Manunda* was damaged, *Peary* was sunk, the RAN lost a lugger and a supply hulk; the Catalinas were destroyed (the Qantas flying-boat was safely screened by smoke from a burning ship) and, when the raiders had flown out to sea, a burning ship at the wharf was blown to pieces by its cargo of depth-charges. Two hours later, formations of high-level land-based Japanese bombers swung in from opposite directions, and when they appeared to merge together over the RAAF base they released their bombs. Main hangars, stores, huts and sheds were destroyed or damaged. Altogether, civilian and service casualties were 240 killed and

150 wounded. The Japanese lost fifteen aircraft.

Australia believed that the enemy would follow the air attack with a landing by an invasion force, and the people's morale dropped to a very low point. Actually, Nagumo was merely knocking Darwin's naval ships and air force while Japanese troops landed on Timor, the Dutch-Portuguese island 400 miles away to the north-west, where a group of stranded Australians were to continue to fight as guerillas. Australia's nervousness continued until advance battalions of the 6th and 7th Divisions arrived back from the Middle East, a few units going to Darwin and Perth, others to prepare for battle in the northern jungles. There were further air raids against Darwin, Wyndham, the small port and air base at Broome, and the inland stations of Katherine and Daly Waters, but the threat of invasion appeared to have ended and the north was strengthened with RAAF Kittyhawks and an AIF brigade.

Admiral Yamamoto, supreme planner of the Pacific assaults, must have felt that Port Moresby would be a push-over, as so many invasions against lightly-held points had been; he possessed Rabaul as a naval-air base and his transports were free to move almost unhindered throughout most of the western Pacific seas. From Port Moresby, Rabaul and the Solomons (and, when he could take them, New Caledonia, Samoa and Fiji), he could extend air operations against northern Australia, patrol the sealanes of its eastern approaches – a half-hearted way of attempting to

The Japanese advance in the South-West Pacific Area towards Australia

The Japanese attack on Darwin, Northern Australia by carrier- aircraft

cut the country off from American supplies – and, with luck, force Australia out of the war. Yamamoto's confidence was enhanced by the fact that up to 1st May his losses had been only twenty-three warships – none larger than a destroyer – and sixty-seven transports. The navy and army General Staffs made their plans but were always influenced by Yamamoto, chief of the Japanese Combined Fleet. He foresaw that a prolonged struggle with the US would be fatal and the obvious way to hold on to their conquests was to sink the US Navy. To do so he must first destroy the carriers and that was the reason he argued for the capture of more island bases, especially Johnson and Midway, which were within bombing distance of Hawaii, and he argued for fleet operations which would bring out US carriers so that he could sink them.

Annoyingly, a squadron of B-25

Mitchell bombers, led by Lieutenant-Colonel James H Doolittle, raided Tokyo from the carrier *USS Hornet* on 18th April. More annoyingly, the US Navy interfered with Operation MO, the plan to occupy Tulagi, in the Solomons, which was to be used as an extra Japanese base to cover the Port Moresby landing. This called for eleven transports to put ashore the South Seas Army Detachment and a naval landing force; a support group would also establish a base in the Louisiades. The interference was caused by Admiral Chester W Nimitz, Commander-in-Chief of the US Pacific Fleet (CINCPAC) who held an ace card: Naval Intelligence at Hawaii had broken the Japanese naval code (a tougher job than interpreting Cuneiform or Hieroglyphics) and monitors simply listened in to lengthy Japanese discussion concerning their plans which included the movement of one light carrier, guarding transports, and two heavy carriers of a striking force that would soon enter the Coral

Sea; Admiral Inouye was in charge, and CINCPAC accurately reasoned that the Japanese were aiming to take Port Moresby.

Nimitz combined two task forces, centred on *Lexington* and *Yorktown* and their supporting heavy cruisers and destroyers, under admirals Fitch and Fletcher (who was given tactical command), to rendezvous with the Australian cruisers, *Australia* and *Hobart*, under Rear-Admiral Crace who was also given *USS Chicago* and the destroyer *Perkins*. They were ordered to the Coral Sea waters that extend from New Guinea's eastern tip across to New Caledonia and wash the north-east Australian coast – where the carriers refuelled on 1st May. Two days later Fletcher was told that Japanese were landing at Tulagi, which had been a base for refuelling RAAF Catalinas, and on the following morning a strike by *Yorktown*'s dive-bombers damaged an enemy destroyer and sank several minesweepers and barges – a minor victory. The carrier sailed back to rejoin *Lexington*. The Japanese had stopped chattering on radio, and cloud covered the invasion force; they were hard to find. On 6th May both Japanese and Allies heard news of the surrender of the last bastion, Corregidor, in the Philippines; on the following day the sea battle commenced. Scouting aircraft from the Japanese carriers found the US destroyer *Sims* which was the first ship to go down, and the US tanker *Neosho* was fatally bombed. Fletcher had detached Crace's ships to seek interception with the invasion force and the Allied cruisers withstood attacks from both Japanese and, by mistake, American bombers without making contact with the transports. Inouye saw the danger and ordered the invasion transports to turn away until the carrier battle was decided.

Aircraft from both US carriers found a Japanese carrier, *Shoho*, and sank her for the loss of only six US aircraft. Commander Dixon, leader of *Lexing-*ton's Dauntless dive-bombers, radioed his famous report: 'Scratch one flattop!' The action was broken off, contacts lost during manoeuvring and in the overcast weather, and it wasn't until the morning of the 8th that the opposing carriers discovered each other: *Shokaku* and *Zuikaku* versus *Lexington* and *Yorktown*, the Japanese with the advantage of experienced air crews and superior torpedoes. *Shokaku* was set alight and retreated to Truk. Then *Yorktown* was hit and slightly damaged and so was *Lexington*, but her damage, wrought by a torpedo, was fatal when escaping fuel vapours were ignited about an hour after the strike and a series of explosions began to wreck her. That evening she was sunk by torpedoes from the US destroyer *Phelps*. The Americans had lost more ships than the Japanese, who had lost one carrier and another put out of action for some considerable time.

This was the first carrier-versus-carrier battle in naval history and, in a physical sense, could be considered a 'draw'. There was a victory however: the Japanese seaborne approach to Port Moresby was prevented and although the troops in those ships would one day fight Australians and Americans, the vitally important base at the bottom of New Guinea was given a respite. The outcome of the Battle of the Coral Sea also had a cheering effect on the people of Australia who had been expecting a landing much closer to home ever since the bombing of Darwin. Their morale was given a greater boost – and so was that of all the Allies – when four Japanese carriers that had taken part in the attacks on Pearl Harbor and Darwin (although no-one knew which carriers they were at the time) were sunk by *Hornet*, *Enterprise* and *Yorktown* at the Battle of Midway, on 4-5th June. Unfortunately, the gallant *Yorktown* was lost in that spectacular battle. As a result of Midway, the balance of power was somewhat adjusted. The Japanese, however, were still particularly strong in cruisers and destroyers which, as well as guarding transports and merchantmen on invasion missions, could also carry troops.

Frustrated in their attempt to take Moresby by landing at some adjacent beach, the Japanese decided to approach overland from the northern side of New Guinea where, at Lae and Salamaua, they had landed on 8th March to establish bases 200 miles directly north of Moresby. The few RAAF communications men and local volunteers wisely withdrew to the hills to maintain their vigil, watching the enemy prepare an airfield at Lae and send parties of troops along the Markham river valley. The 'eyes' of the Allies were a few reconnaissance aircraft operating from Moresby, Darwin and Townsville, and a remarkable collection of observers scattered around the islands. The Coast-watchers were to prove invaluable in the land, sea and air operations to come, particularly in Papua-New Guinea and the Solomons.

The formation of a coast-watching organization was one of those simple, practical ideas used throughout military history to maintain a personal observation over the enemy; a system enhanced with the development of wireless sets. A naval prerogative, coast watching had been a pleasant, exciting duty for sea-scouts in Britain during the First World War; guarding beaches and spotting trawler movements, damaged seaplanes, floating mines and Zeppelin flights. Those boys were at play near the edge of war: for adults coast-watching in the Pacific Islands it was a game of life and death, one of the most unpleasant and dangerous full-time duties. There had already been a war in New Guinea when, in 1914, a small Australian force defeated a small force of Germans in what was then their mandated territory. At the end of that war, the RAN formed a coast watching organization among civilians on the mainland, providing the nucleus of an observation unit for any future military or naval emergency. Later, the Navy extended the service to New Guinea and the Solomons and, by 1939, there were some 700 planters, officials and servicemen trained in the rudiments

The aircraft-carriers *Soryu* (*above*) and *Hiryu* (*opposite*), part of the Japanese task force that attacked Darwin, Northern Australia. Both ships were later sunk at the Battle of Midway, 4th June 1943

of observation and reporting. When war came again to the Pacific, Eric Feldt, an ex-RAN lieutenant-commander who had been a government district officer in New Guinea, was appointed by Naval Intelligence to take over the Coast Watchers. Civilian members were enlisted into the RAN or one of the other services so that they would not be treated as spies should they be captured; unfortunately they were, in any case, doomed to execution if they fell into the hands of the enemy, the eventual fate of too many of those very courageous men. Coast-watchers covered every strait and passage from San Cristobal in the south Solomons right around the top of New Guinea to the Admiralty Islands, as well as covering all the major points of Papua – New Guinea. As the Japanese made their various landings and intrusions, the chain was partly broken, the watchers either escaping or being captured in the process.

New Britain, quite a large island, had small European settlements at Arawe, Gasmata and Talasea, as well as at the volcano-hill town of Rabaul. Inland, the country was rough and wild, a suitable place for watching and hiding and the watchers were able to describe events as they happened there. At Salamaua across the Huon Gulf from Lae, in New Guinea,

RAAF radar screens, Vial's advance notices of raids were invaluable to the Kittyhawk fighter pilots making interceptions, and to the Army ack-ack gunners protecting the strips and the harbour. The Vial warning system operated for six months until he was relieved. Old New Guinea hands were the only people who could perform this job well, because they spoke the language of the natives and knew how to live off the land. Men like Vial made it possible for Moresby to survive the onslaughts that were to come from enemy fighters from Lae and from Rabaul-based bombers. If the RAAF, and later the USAAF, defences had been blasted from Moresby, the enemy might have been tempted to make another sea-borne attack.

The world's largest island, New Guinea had been sparsely settled by Europeans since its first discovery by unknown voyagers centuries ago. In 1512, two Portugese sailors landed on the eastern part which they named Ilhas dos Papuas – islands of people with crinkly hair. In 1545, Ynigo Ortisde Retoz, a Spaniard, landed on

there were high hills which gave cover and excellent observation positions from where an assistant district officer, L G Vial, could report all enemy flights from Lae. Since the hills behind Moresby blanketed the

the eastern tip and named that area New Guinea because it reminded him of the Guinea coast of Africa (or possibly because that was where he thought he actually was). Over the succeeding centuries few visitors

Admiral Shushin Nagano, head of the Japanese General Naval Staff

Admiral Isoroku Yamamoto, supreme planner of Japanese Pacific assaults

stayed long or ventured inland, the natives being too accurate with arrows and stone axes, and it wasn't until the middle 19th century that gun-equipped explorers moved into the country. They found the people to be keen traders but murderous if they thought their rights were being violated. Even in the 1950s there were isolated villages where white men had never been seen and, when they were contacted, some warrior chiefs felt so defenceless against armed patrol officers, so impotent in not being able to remain complete lords of their districts in the face of possible violation of their rights, that they vomited with rage.

In Europe's 1880s rush to colonise, Britain claimed south-east New Guinea, Holland the western half and Germany annexed north-east New Guinea (Kaiser Wilhelmsland), New Britain (Neu Pommern), New Ireland (Neu Mecklenberg) and other smaller islands. In the 1914–18 war Australians wrested these territories from the Germans in a few skirmishes; after the war the League of Nations gave Australia a mandate to administer the Territories of Papua and New Guinea. Discovery of gold in the 1930s brought

many prospectors and investors into the land where most of the already established Europeans were missionaries. In 1920 the Australian Parliament passed the New Guinea Act, under which the government would 'promote to the utmost the material and moral well-being and social progress of the inhabitants of the territory'. Compared with most colonised primitive countries, the natives of New Guinea were not exploited and were treated with sympathy and understanding by patrol officers and district officers of the Administration, which faced a difficult task introducing western justice to stone-age feudalism.

The Melanesian tribes lived in great isolation, as some still do, in rugged mountains, high valley plateaux and swampy coastal plains. Man was there 50,000 years ago and a new immigration took place some 5,000 years ago when, possibly, people from Indonesia arrived during a 'Neolithic revolution', bringing taro, yam, banana, coconut, pigs, dogs and chickens to supplement the local produce of sago-palm, sugar cane and kinds of banana and breadfruit. Local fauna are various types of marsupial, notably tree-

Lieutenant-Colonel James H Doolittle and his crew (with Chinese friends) of one of the B-25 Mitchells which raided Tokyo from the carrier *USS Hornet*

kangaroo, seventy kinds of snake – including taipan, death adder and ringed coral snake – crocodiles, and myriads of insects – scorpions, centipedes, ants, sandflies, typhus-bearing mites and malaria-carrying mosquitoes. In this creepy-crawly paradise are some of the world's most beautiful butterflies and birds. The best eating bird is the large, crested pigeon and the worst is the tall cassowary which, it is claimed, should be cooked with a stone in the pot: when the stone is ready to eat so is the cassowary.

Warriors or wealthy garden owners or clever sorcerers were chiefs of villages of 100 to 300 people, or of family hamlets. There were also single, isolated homes built of palms on pole frameworks. Developed from their original stock language are a group of languages with subsidiary area dialects and the *lingua franca*, spread by natives who worked with patrol officers or traders, is pidgin English. The words themselves are easily understood but spoken in fast, word-connected sentences the sense is quite difficult to pick up. For example, when Rabaul was taken from the Germans in 1914, the proclamation went like this:

'All boys belonga one place, you savvy big master he come now, he new feller master, he strong feller too much, you look him all ships stop place . . . You look him new feller plag (flag); you savvy him? He belonga British . . . he look out good alonga you; he give good feller kai-kai (food; eat) . . . You no fight other feller black man other feller place, you no kai-kai man . . . Me been talk alonga you now, now you give three goodfeller cheers belonga new feller master. No more 'um Kaiser. God Save Um King'. This seemingly joke-language, despite its small trade-origin vocabulary of English, Melanesian and some German words, was an essential language for the Allies – and Japanese – to understand in their recruitment of thousands of carriers during the New Guinea operations. In the early part of the campaign, human transport won for the Allies the battle of the supply lines. Australians, Americans and Japanese learned pidgin – and so did the wild-looking tribesmen recruited from remote mountain ridges and valleys. There were some people in the central and western highlands who saw nothing of the war – or of white men – while others suffered

The Japanese aircraft-carrier *Shoho* (*above*) torpedoed at the Battle of the Coral Sea and the *USS Lexington* (*below*) also sinking after the engagement. The *USS Yorktown* (*bottom*) was in the same task force as *Lexington*

under Japanese occupation and from battle action. The Japanese were complete foreigners to them, mistrusted at first and soon feared and hated for their ruthlessness.

Papua–New Guinea, the island's eastern area where most of the fighting took place, is up to 600 miles across and 1,000 miles long. Snow falls on the highest mountains which rise up to 15,400 feet in a long central range, branching out in a series of coastal ranges. On the coast there are many tidal, crocodile-infested swamps where villages are constructed on stilts; from the foothills up to 6,000 feet grow thick rain forests with dense canopies shutting out sunlight from the undergrowth of lawyer vine and creepers that can form an impenetrable barrier; above 11,000 feet the trees are mainly small conifers and above 13,000 feet thick moss and grasses grow in the cold air. On the southern side, in the Port Moresby area, is an unusual dry pocket where types of eucalyptus grow, whereas in the mountains and on the northern coast it rains even in the 'dry' season; when the North-West monsoons come down, and then the South-East trades, the rain never seems to stop. Moresby is wet from January to about April, after which it is reliably dry and dusty.

This inhospitable, stone-age land of tropical diseases and appalling climate was the setting for a campaign that would cost the Japanese 100,000 lives. And it was the Japanese who chose to campaign there, to defend their occupation and to fight to the last sick and starved man.

It was obvious to the Allies that Port Moresby was just as important to them as to the Japanese; it was the logical base for defensive and offensive operations and could be as effectively used by one side as the other for such purposes. The capital of the Territory of Papua might have been developed as a base much earlier had the facts of Singapore's vulnerability been examined more closely.

The Moresby defences were appallingly weak: there was a coast defence battery, a brigade of young militiamen and part of a field artillery regiment; their available numbers were reduced through dysentery in the first month, then malaria and dengue inflicted more casualties. Many of them drafted, some of them volunteers, the troops' average age was nineteen; they had been given little training and their morale was low. After Rabaul fell on 23rd January, Moresby's commandant, Major-General Basil Morris, had a panicky native population on his hands. 600 European women and children had been evacuated from the Territories and all 'able-bodied white males' were called up for military service.

The native inhabitants of the town may not have known why the Japanese were invading New Guinea but they certainly knew that the dangers were very real. Raids by aircraft from Rabaul or from carriers were expected and their pilots knew that the defences were not strong. The RAAF had a few Catalina flying-boats, Hudson bombers and Wirraway – NA-33, Harvard – trainers to defend all the islands and no-one, not even the Commandant, knew if aircraft reserves would ever be brought up. Before the Coral Sea battle, before it was known that USN carriers could be available for use against sea-borne invasions, and before any concrete plans about strengthening Moresby were announced, Japanese bombs were dropped – on 3rd February. When a false alarm sounded the natives fled and stayed away for up to two days; when the bombs did fall, they went bush – from jobs in the town, from coastal ships and from prisons (with their warders). When invasions, which were expected after each bombing, did not eventuate, desertions to the bush became fewer, although both natives and whites took to sleeping away from the town. Morale among civilians and troops improved when Squadron Leader John Jackson led in his No 75 Squadron, RAAF, of P-40 Kittyhawks. They were fired on by garrison anti-aircraft gunners who expected any large, low-flying flights of aircraft to be Japanese; the troops stopped firing and whooped with enthusiasm when two of the Kittyhawks shot down a Jap twin-engined recce plane into the harbour.

However, one squadron of Kittyhawks and the 30th Brigade of militia could not possibly be a deterrent to one or more full-scale invasions which the Japanese could mount on the northern, eastern or southern coasts of the two Territories; in fact the defenders were not mobile and were virtually stuck at Moresby, awaiting invasion and prepared to retreat into the hills if the enemy landed in force. The Kittyhawks successfully challenged the Zeros and bombers overhead, and raided the enemy 'Lae Wing' at their strip on the north coast. Hudsons, Catalinas and the occasional B-17 from Townsville reconnoitred, and the infantry trained.

Brigadier S H W C Porter, a former AIF battalion commander, came up to take over the brigade and Morris took over general administration, including the military organization of native affairs – the Australian New Guinea Administrative Unit (Angau). Having commanded the 2/31st Battalion in Syria, Porter probably felt despair after meeting the poorly trained, dispirited troops of 30th Brigade. He sent for experienced officers and NCOs from AIF groups in Australia to bolster his new command and intensified training, but they were nowhere near ready when General Blamey signalled that 'a serious attack against you and the troops under your command will develop in the immediate future'. That was on 8th May, when Pilot Officer Pennycuik radioed from his Hudson that an enemy carrier was escorting transports sailing towards Moresby, the report that brought Allied ships into action in the Coral Sea.

General Horii's three-pronged seaborne attack on Moresby was postponed. Plump and small, sitting like

The cruisers *HMAS Australia* (*below*) and *USS Chicago* (*opposite*) under Rear-Admiral J C Crace at the Battle of the Coral Sea 7/8th May 1942

a bespectacled doll, Emperor-style, on his white horse, Horii had led troops in China, at Guam, Rabaul and Salamau. It is not known if he disapproved of his troops massacring with bayonets Australian prisoners tied to the trunks of coconut palms, an outrage committed after the fall of Rabaul. Other luckless prisoners from that garrison had perished when their prison ship, *Montevideo Maru,* was torpedoed by an American submarine. Under the command of Major-General Tomitaro, Horii's South Seas Detached Force (*Nankai Shitai*), experienced and so far victorious, sailed back to Rabaul to await Yamamoto's next decision regarding Moresby. His Lae Wing continued their battle and suffered greater losses against the Kittyhawk squadron. The Australians were down to their last few fighters when USAAF P-39 squadrons came on the scene. In 44 days they had destroyed 50 enemy aircraft for the loss of 22 Kittyhawks and 12 pilots. (See *Pacific Hawk*, Weapons Book No 14 in this series.) Yamamoto rightly believed that a sea approach was the quickest and surest way to take Moresby but the Battle of Midway was

to spoil that tactic and he eventually decided to make a two-pronged cross-country attack: to land at Buna, about one hundred air miles away from Moresby on the northern coast, and at Milne Bay, about 175 miles away to the east. (See map.) From Buna, the approach would be over the Owen Stanley Range, and from Milne Bay he would stage along the coast. Meanwhile, the opposing forces were gathering strength and the battle for Japan itself was about to begin, thousands of miles from the homeland, at the bottom of the South West Pacific – at Guadalcanal, Milne Bay and across the New Guinea highlands.

A whole programme for large-scale defence and offence was being worked out by the Allies in Washington and Melbourne (Australia's military headquarters). Moresby and Horn Island airfields were to be extended and new ones constructed at Mareeba, Cooktown and Coen in north Queensland. Two of the three Australian AIF divisions had returned or were on their way from the Middle East to be readied for the tropics.

Returning to the scene of his defeat

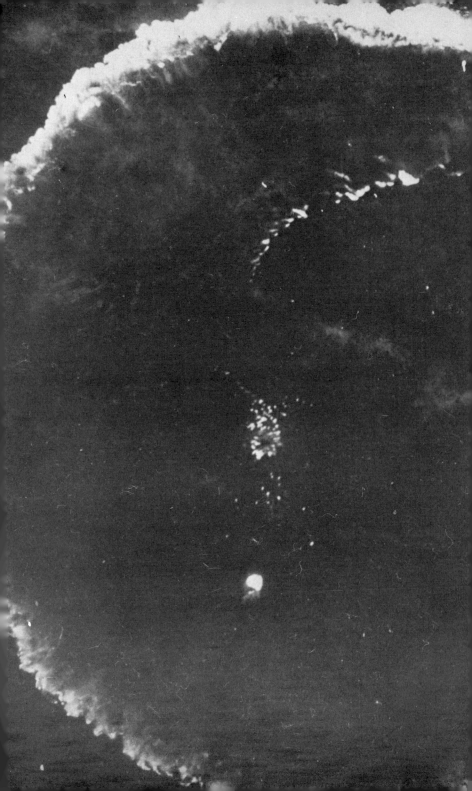

The Japanese carrier *Soryu* avoids
attack at Battle of Midway

seemed to be the main objective for
MacArthur and had some effect on his
overall strategic plans when he was
made Supreme Commander – or Commander-in-Chief, the title he preferred – of the South West Pacific
Area. Brigadier-General Dwight D
Eisenhower, one of the US Army's
most respected planners, had advised
General Marshall to establish an
advanced base in Australia with some
troops and supplies which had already
been diverted to Brisbane in December.

General George H Brett was selected
to command the USAAF in Australia,
and fighters and bombers were promised. General Wavell, Allied Commander in Java, thought that the
United States would come to the aid
of Australia and that the Middle East
AIF veterans should be sent to Java,
a plan sponsored by Churchill and
Roosevelt. Prime Minister John
Curtin exchanged some very strongly
worded messages on the subject of
where the AIF should be sent, causing
bitter feelings in what Churchill later
described as 'a painful episode' that
developed in political and military
circles in London. Politicians might
want to fight wars without generals
and generals without politicians: inevitably there is a clash of opinions
regarding strategy and priorities, and
about who should be leader in the field.
In February, Churchill and Roosevelt
agreed that Britain should be responsible for the Indian Ocean theatre
and America for the 'right flank' of
the Pacific. The war generally was to
be directed by their Combined Chiefs
of Staff, while the United States Joint
Chiefs of Staff were to exercise operational control in the Pacific: the SWPA
was to be an Army responsibility and
the Pacific Ocean Area the Navy's,
with General Marshall and Admiral
King as their Chiefs. With these
decisions made, Prime Minister Curtin
was content to receive MacArthur as
commander in Australia; the build-up

The carrier *USS Yorktown* (*above*) unable to manoeuvre after first Japanese torpedo attack and (*below*) hit by further Japanese air attacks

of forces would thereby be guaranteed. The only thing known by the public was that he seemed impressive in the extensive press coverage. Everything supplied by Australia to Americans, and all the armaments and equipment they brought for use by Australians, would be accounted for in the Lease-Lend arrangement.

By June, the ground forces available were 104,000 AIF, 265,000 militia and 38,000 Americans; very few were trained front-line troops. The returned AIF battalion, brigade and divisional commanders may not have had tropical battle experience but they had fought Italians, Germans and Vichy-French, and it was expected that senior officers would be appointed to MacArthur's staff. But no. Even though General Marshall requested him to do so, MacArthur asserted that there were no qualified senior Australian – or Dutch – officers available and he filled senior positions with Americans, all of whom, except three, had been with him in the Philippines. He also wanted an American general to take command of the land forces but Washington was satisfied with the appointment of the Australian Middle East commander, General Sir Thomas Blamey.

Tom Blamey had been chief of staff to General Sir John Monash, an outstanding AIF leader in the First War, who wrote of him: 'he possessed a mind cultured far above the average, widely informed, alert and prehensible (sic). After that war Blamey was appointed Victoria's Chief Commissioner of Police, resigning after a few years as a result of an adverse finding by a Royal Commission appointed to investigate the circumstances surrounding the shooting of one of his superintendents. As a result, he was out in the cold, and he was left there until the Munich madness alerted the Australian government to make preparations for a possible war. When the formation of a Second AIF was planned, the government was influenced to consider Blamey as its

commander, not because ex-soldier parliamentarians such as Sir Henry Gullett and Richard Casey were particular sponsors, but because there was no better man available.

Unlike the tall, lean, typical Australian staff officer, Blamey was a shortish five feet six and a half inches and solidly built. He was appointed GSO III (Intelligence) under Bridges' 1st Division in 1915 after having worked in the Intelligence Branch of the War Office; he was in England when war broke out in 1914. He went ashore at Gallipoli a few days after the landing and, except for brief periods of battalion and brigade commands, had been completely involved in planning during the First World War: as GSO III and GSO I of the 1st Division, and in 1918 as Monash's chief of staff. Monash's high reputation was partly built on the excellence of the work carried out by his staff officers; if Blamey had stepped into his shoes in 1918 it is highly probable that achievements of the Corps in France would have been as great. Blamey is said to have originated the idea that led to the Battle of Amiens, the beginning of the end of the Great War; Blamey had discussed the idea with Monash and they both believed, against the hesitation of Foch and British higher commanders, that the deterioration on the German front provided an opportunity for a great offensive and breakthrough to shatter the Hindenburg Line. Spearheaded by the Australian and Canadian corps, this offensive succeeded and led to the Armistice three months later. It was, therefore, a wise decision to choose him to lead the AIF in the Second World War.

Monash wrote of Blamey: 'Some day the series of orders which he drafted for the long series of history-making military operations, upon which we collaborated, will become a model for staff Colleges and Schools for military instruction. They were accurate, lucid in language, perfect in detail, and always an exact interpretation of my intention. It was seldom that I thought my orders or instructions could have been better expressed'. Yet his ruthless determination to succeed was in the true tradition of those inheriting the 'Napoleon complex'; a difficult obstacle for both friend and foe to overcome – they simply had to accept it.

In Greece he was GOC of the Anzac Corps, the two divisions of Australians and New Zealanders joined together for the first and last time as a corps in the Second World War, although an Australian division and a New Zealand division fought with the Eighth Army at El Alamein. Blamey was astute enough to see that assistance to mainland Greece was a hopeless gesture and he was against the campaign from the beginning, preferring to make a more determined stand on Crete and Rhodes.

After Greece, Blamey was appointed Deputy C-in-C in the Middle East and retained his position as GOC, AIF. Visiting Australia in November 1941,

he called at Malaya where he was troubled by the atmosphere of 'Indian Garrison' life that he saw during his brief visit. In Australia, he told Australians they were 'a lot of gazelles in a dell on the edge of a jungle', that they did not realise the seriousness of the war of survival against Germany. They did not accept Blamey's views until the 'yellow peril' made war a reality.

The Japanese thrust was so violently successful that, after Malaya fell, Chief of the General Staff Sturdee advised the Prime Minister that there was only a 'sporting chance' of defending the country, even if the AIF were brought home. The loss of the 8th Division in Malaya had been a serious blow. Soon after the bombing of Darwin Blamey had been recalled.

Fire-fighting on the carrier *USS Enterprise* (*below*) which survived the Battle of Midway unlike the Japanese carrier *Hiryu* (*opposite, top*) and cruiser *Mikuma* (*opposite, bottom*)

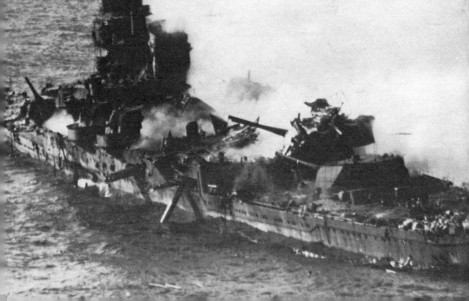

Above: US troops, speaking 'pidgin English' obtain intelligence reports about Japanese movements from a local Papuan. *Below:* Port Moresby ; the last major Allied base held after the Japanese invasion of New Guinea. General Douglas MacArthur, Supreme Commander SWPA with General Sir Thomas Blamey

With aerial communications interrupted, he flew to South Africa where he boarded the *Queen Mary*, and en route he heard the news broadcast that MacArthur had been appointed Supreme Commander in the South West Pacific Area. His reaction was quoted in *Blamey*, by John Hetherington: 'I think that's the best thing that could have happened for Australia ... MacArthur will be so far away from his own government that he won't have any interference from them, and as far as our own government is concerned he won't take any notice of them'. Despite his sympathy for another general who might be henpecked by politicians, Blamey must have felt disappointed at the decision, yet he realised even then that it was a sound political move, for American forces were urgently needed and an American figurehead would not be unpopular with Australian troops. He admired MacArthur's military gifts. At times he was to be in conflict with MacArthur's egocentric will and one day he was to admit, 'The best and the worst things you hear about him [MacArthur] are both true'.

The First Australian Imperial Force, which began to form the day Australia declared war in 1914, provided five divisions, and when the Second AIF was formed in 1939, the division numbers began at six; thus the first battalion of the Second AIF was the 2/1st Battalion of the 16th Brigade, 6th Division. The shoulder colour patches for each unit remained the same except that they were edged with grey to denote Second AIF. The Militia divisions numbered from 1st Division (a training unit) and were filled with both volunteers and conscripts. Between wars, militiamen trained at weekends and spent a fortnight in camp each year and from their ranks came practically all the officers and NCOs of the AIF volunteer force. The rate of pay for a private soldier was five shillings a day, plus a shilling deferred until his discharge, plus allowances for married men and their families; the rate was raised another shilling in 1942.

Land fighting begins

At home, morale had improved after the shaking events at Darwin and Rabaul. When a midget submarine sneaked under the Sydney Harbour boom and, missing *USS Chicago* with the lethal part of a torpedo salvo, destroyed an old naval ferry boat, there was no panic. When Newcastle and Sydney were hit by a few shells fired haphazardly from another submarine, there were very few people who left their homes to stay with friends in the country, and there were fewer still who sent supplies of canned food to Alice Springs where

they expected to quake in safety. As more and more AIF and RAAF returned there was confidence that the Japs would get nowhere if they tried to invade. The Armoured Division – the only one – was getting its tanks, replacement Kittyhawks and more Americans were arriving with bombers and fighters, and there was the AIF 9th Division in the Middle East – a solid reserve if they survived against Rommel. The locally made Boomerang fighter could actually get off the ground and fly at 'about' 300 miles per hour, bombers would also be built and

Australian guerillas on Timor (*opposite*) in tactically ideal country. Though their appearance was unorthodox (*above*) they tied down many Japanese

a young man named Evelyn Owen had invented a light-weight machine gun that could stand up to wet, muddy, tropical conditions. Rifles, machine-guns, mortars, artillery and ammunition were already being produced at a satisfactory rate in local factories, and the government's manpower organization looked after production. Food rationing never became unbear-able for civilians, while the troops, especially Americans, lived on a healthy and plentiful diet. Except, of course, as always happens, in the front line.

As both sides looked at their equipment and reserves, guerilla skirmishes began in the Markham Valley and in the Owen Stanley Range.

A Lancashire man, Corporal (later Major) J B McAdam was a forestry officer and a member of the New Guinea Volunteer Rifles when he was recruited as a coast watcher outside Salamaua. He later described how they avoided the Japs who began hunting them within a month of landing: 'We used only our own tracks and we took pains never to mark the main tracks so that, whenever we saw them, they were a book telling us what the Japs had been doing. Our tracks were so lightly marked that it took a good bushman to find them. We left no marks in that forward country. We walked carefully on roots, stones. We had the heels taken off our boots. Where necessary we walked our natives behind us to put their tracks over ours... in forward scouting pairs, we took a pistol each, the good one and the uncertain one. Our sole defence was our speed. We could see a Jap before he could see us and if we had ten yards' start we could get away... All the four months I was there we were unable to get a Tommy-gun. There were about six in the NGVR but we didn't have one'. Natives living near his first camp suffered for helping them and McAdam changed his camp to avoid further trouble for them.

Around Lae there were, as well as coast watchers, members of NGVR keen to harass the enemy. Corporal Clark walked into Lae for a closer inspection, circled the airfield and brought back tags from bombs as evidence of his reconnaissance. The Markham Valley was obviously an ideal place to begin operations with some of the AIF Commandos of which there were, by now, eight companies formed, three of them fully trained. The 2/1st Independent Company was spread from the Admiralties to the New Hebrides, 2/2nd was on Timor, 2/3rd on New Caledonia, 2/4th in the Northern Territory, and 2/5th was sent to Port Moresby for the Markham operation. On 23rd May that company, a mortar detachment and the head-quarters of the little group called Kanga Force, under the command of Major N L Fleay, were carried by air transport to Wau where they picked up a platoon of riflemen, part of two companies of NGVR. Kanga Force

now comprised 450 fit newcomers and 250 weary NGVR.

They planned an attack on Sala-maua. To begin, they studied the place at such close range it could have been a friendly village, they reconnoitered every track out of it, and they chose the aerodrome, supply dumps and wireless station as primary targets. A Scots planter from Java, Captain N I Winning, led the four-platoon night raid on 28th June. They blew up or shot Japs in huts and at defensive positions, altogether about a hundred; they destroyed three trucks and a bridge, and they brought back some bits of Japanese equipment and some maps, orders and a diary. For an attack on Lae, two NGVR men had a bright idea: they would float on a raft down the Markham at night to near Lae and sabotage the aerodrome; however, the raft could not be brought close to the bank and, being in danger of floating by in full sight of the enemy, they capsized the raft to destroy their stores, swam ashore and walked back. Other raids successfully inflicted casualties among the enemy for the loss of very few Kanga Force men. Eventually, the supply position worsened through lack of aircraft, a situation which was to hamper operations during the early months of the campaign. Threatened by Japanese, native carriers were becoming afraid to work for the Australians, and the life of an ill-fed guerilla was not conducive to high morale. So, when a transport ship landed more enemy and supplies at Salamaua, and when, in August, about a thousand troops made a three-pronged move towards his base at Mubo, Major Fleay moved back through wild Kukukuku country (and wild Kukukuku people) to the head of the Bulldog Track. Bulolo and Wau were virtually offered to an enemy who was nervous and suspicious and who delayed too long in taking over the deserted village and airstrip of Wau.

A native pad (path), used for centuries as a communicating link between

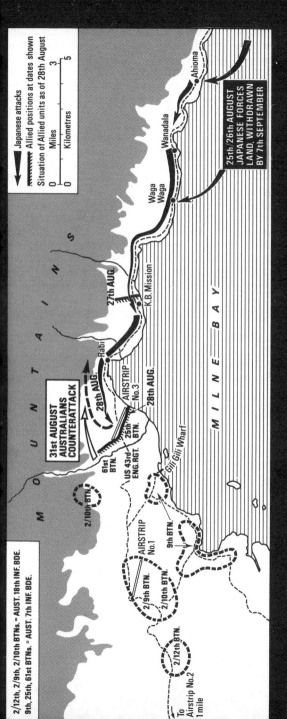

Milne Bay. The Japanese failure to outflank Port Moresby

Map labels and legend:

2/12th, 2/9th, 2/10th BTNs. = AUST. 18th INF. BDE.
9th, 25th, 61st BTNs. = AUST. 7th INF. BDE.

Legend:
Japanese attacks
Allied positions at dates shown
Situation of Allied units as of 28th August

Miles 0 — 3
Kilometres 0 — 5

MOUNTAINS

27th AUG

K.B. Mission

Rabi

28th AUG.

31st AUGUST
AUSTRALIANS
COUNTERATTACK

28th AUG.

AIRSTRIP No.3

61st BTN.

25th BTN.

US 43rd ENG. RGT.

Gili Gili Wharf

M I L N E   B A Y

Waga Waga

Wanadala

Ahioma

25th/26th AUGUST
JAPANESE FORCES
LAND, WITHDRAWN
BY 7th SEPTEMBER

2/10th BTN.

AIRSTRIP No.1

2/9th BTN.

2/10th BTN.

9th BTN.

2/12th BTN.

To
Airstrip No.2
1 mile

tribes on both sides of the Owen Stanleys, was the main Japanese invasion passage. They had mapped it in their plans before they landed on the New Guinea coast, but they may not have known what a difficult track it was. Australians knew that distances along this primitive route were not counted in miles but in hours of climbing and clambering, sometimes walking and sometimes crawling; from Buna and from Moresby the winding path was junctioned halfway across at the village and airfield of Kokoda and was therefore called the Kokoda Track. There was no possibility of taking any vehicle along the track; it was formed by feet and that was the only way it could be traversed – along its ridges, valleys, hills, mountains, through its jungles and across its streams – by footslogging.

Milne Bay and Buna were coveted as future bases by both Japanese and Allies. Disregarding warnings that the Buna-Gona area would be occupied first by the enemy, GHQ made their plans to move there a few days after Marines were to land on Guadalcanal in early August. One of the New Guinea objectives was to establish an all-weather air-strip on the grass plains fifteen miles south of Buna – at Dobodura – for an offensive against the Japanese at Lae and Salamaua. Grabbing their opportunity, 1,800 Japanese troops landed between Buna and Gona on the night of 21st–22nd July, having safely survived attacks on their transports by Fortresses and Marauders. Allied bombing during this period was quite woeful. Fortunately, the Allies were luckier at Milne Bay, getting there first with the 7th Brigade of militiamen and a force of US engineers who established defence positions and began scraping away coconut palms to construct airstrips. One was ready in early August to accommodate two RAAF Kittyhawk squadrons and a few Hudson reconnaissance-bombers.

As the 7th Brigade moved into

Left: Visual evidence of US support;
USS Chicago in Wooloomooloo Bay
Above: The lifeline of both Allies and
Japanese; Papuan carriers resting

Milne Bay under Brigadier Field, its only officer who had had experience in the current war, a small detachment, Maroubra Force, was sent out from Moresby along the trail beyond Kokoda on a reconnaissance mission. They were in a position overlooking the northern coastal plain, over Buna and Gona and the sea beyond, when the Japanese landed. Colonel Yokoyama, an engineer officer, led a reconnaissance party up their side of the Kokoda Track to inspect the path which might lead Horii's army to Moresby. Their movement was challenged by Australian militiamen who were forced back rather rapidly, the experienced Japanese infiltrating and outflanking the inexperienced opposition until, by the end of the

month, Kokoda village and its airfield were taken. Having done so well in only seven days and with a comparatively small force, Japanese Seventeenth Army HQ ordered Horii to take further advantage of the success and the apparent weakness of the Australians to make a definite attack along the old native trail. Kokoda became the enemy's forward base and supplies and reinforcements were brought up. More troops were brought across from Rabaul.

This was an ideal time for General Hyakutake, the Seventeenth Army commander, to set in motion the second phase of his two-pronged attack on Port Moresby and send an assault force into Milne Bay. However, he received two shocks that nevertheless did not stop his operation, although the first reduced the number of troops he could employ in New Guinea. Major-General Vandergrift's 1st Marine Division landed at Guadal-

**CAC Boomerang A45-2s were
Australia's answer to the Japanese Zero**

canal and took Henderson Field – an unexpected offensive which Hyakutake had not considered could take place so soon – and Milne Bay was already occupied by the Allies. Off the south-east tip of Papua is a small island that had appealed to Hyakutake because of its position and name – Samarai – and which he had planned to occupy as well, but now he would have to concentrate his forces on whoever had constructed and fortified that airstrip at Milne Bay. As a security measure, radios of the RAAF Kittyhawks had been silent since their arrival, until 4th August when a patrol of five encountered four Zeros and a dive-bomber, the dive-bomber being shot down. One of the Zeros had its wheels down – the Japanese pilot may have thought that the base was one of theirs. The Zeros escaped the Kittyhawks and doubtless were the first to report on the Milne Bay

development. On 26th August, the Japanese launched a general offensive on the Kokoda Track and despatched barges and ships loaded with troops to take Milne Bay.

On the afternoon of the 4th August the battalion was carrying out an exercise on their Queensland camping grounds when Driver J Ferguson came out in the staff car bearing a message from the brigadier, who required the CO at brigade headquarters. On the journey this conversation took place:
Ferguson: "This is it, sir."
The CO: "This is what?"
Ferguson: "We'll be moving, sir."
The CO: "Moving where?"
Ferguson: "New Guinea, sir."
The CO: "How the hell do you know?"
Ferguson: "I got it from one of the cooks at Division, sir."
The CO: "Then it must be right.'"

This is quoted from the history of the AIF 2/10th Battalion and is one true example of the origin of rumours. The 2/10th did go to New Guinea, as rumoured, with the 2/9th and 2/12th who made up the 18th Brigade. With them went the militia 7th Brigade, made up of Queenslanders of the 9th, 25th and 61st Battalions, whose commander, Brigadier Field, was once CO of the 2/12th. When they landed, in early August, the ground was firm enough for trucks to carry them along the road near the edge of the bay, past the airstrip laid with metal plates, to the camp area. The roads did not last long; they were formed of soft coral which broke up under the movement of vehicles, so the men were employed to manhandle equipment and stores. At first there were intervals of clear sky, although the rain, when it fell, was heavy. The airstrip had been constructed by 43rd US Engineer Regiment and 24th Field Company, militia; a second airstrip was being cleared and defence positions dug. The infantry also worked on the defences.

From an opening seven miles wide at a strait called China, Milne Bay was twenty miles long, from east to west, and on the western shores was a large coconut plantation – Gili Gili – around which were heavily wooded mountains. There was a track all the way around the bay, a muddy, not completely cleared track that was never further than a hundred yards from mangrove swamps by the sea and, on the northern side, it ran close to the foot of steep, bush-covered country cut by several creeks. The northern side of the bay, suitable for landing, had place names: Ahioma, Waga Waga, Goroni, K B Mission and Rabi; and, closer to Gili Gili wharf, was the long Number 3 strip, cleared of trees but not yet surfaced for use. At the wharf was a supply vessel, *Anshun*, and the hospital ship *Manunda* had been brought into the bay to receive wounded. In a direct line north of Rabi, about six air miles away on the coast of Goodenough Bay, was another suitable landing place – Taupota.

The troops' food was the usual tinned 'bully beef', M and V (meat and vegetables), tinned fruit, hard biscuits and lots of tea. Yeast had been forgotten in the move, so the cooks substituted fermented coconut milk and turned out a reasonable loaf of bread. In later Pacific campaigns, coconut milk was to be used to make an illicit alcoholic beverage called jungle-juice. Some brews were quite drinkable. Coconuts however were also dangerous. A five-pound nut falling sixty feet from a tree – and this was all plantation area – could kill a man. After a senior officer was hit on his shoulder everyone was ordered to wear his tin helmet. On an exercise a platoon commander reported back to his company, 'Am bravely carrying on despite coconut fire.' The nut's juice and meat was nevertheless a welcome addition to the soldiers' monotonous diet.

Almost as soon as they arrived, troops were going down with tropical diseases. A later investigation showed that lines across a malaria-rainfall graph were parallel – the higher the rainfall during a fortnight or a month, the higher the incidence of malaria. In the June-December period, the incidence could be 100 cases per 1,000 soldiers per week! And during the Milne Bay fighting, the rain rarely stopped. The troops were issued with quinine which, unfortunately, suppressed the symptoms if a soldier had the disease, and if he were used as a blood donor to a wounded man, the malaria was passed on – without the aid of a mosquito's little hypodermic nose. Quinine came from Java and was scarce; American-developed Atabrin replaced the drug. A fine of £3 was imposed on men walking barefoot, because the native tracks were infested with hook-worm. Queensland shorts were changed to tropical long pants and the men were told to avoid scratches which could soon turn into tropical sores. The small, functional green mosquito net had not then been on issue, only the large white type that could be seen for miles. The local natives, who were very friendly and

Above: Supplies for Karga Force being landed for onward movement by canoe to Bulldog Camp. *Below:* Elements of Kanga Force move out to attack the Japanese

lived in a small collection of hut-hamlets, taught the troops how to build small sleeping platforms with a roof of plaited coconut leaves. To satisfy the Diggers' fetish for cleanliness, there were numerous nearby streams for bathing and washing clothes.

Before the crunch at Milne Bay, people with the toughest job were the fighter pilots of 75 and 76 Squadrons and the crews of a flight of 6 Squadron Hudson reconnaissance-bombers, without whom (as is shown more fully in *Pacific Hawk*) the enemy would have taken a permanent foothold. The pilots' living conditions were hardly any better than those of the troops, and the strip from which they operated was a quagmire with a steel-mesh base. When a Kittyhawk landed, it threw out a spray of mud that caked on the fuselage and tail surfaces, and the landing itself always provided an incipent ground-skid. 75 Squadron had held the fort at Moresby; both squadrons' leaders and most of the pilots were veterans, and they were inspired by the fact that it was their responsibility to work closely with Australian soldiers, an odd brotherly quirk of morale that worked equally strongly on the troops. They placed a great trust in each other, a valuable asset when both were about to test themselves for the first time against an invading, so-called invincible enemy. There was no chance of evacuation when he came – the Jap controlled the seas here – and it was a long hike back to Moresby. The Number 1 strip, of course, would be the first Japanese objective after they established their beach-head. And being only a couple of miles inland from the beach at the middle of the western end of the bay, the fighting would be close to it wherever they landed. The decision of chance in that detail was uppermost in the mind of Major-General Clowes: where would the Japs land if they invaded?

The Second AIF appointed First World War veterans to command battalions and to higher commands for the early formations. Most of these officers were civilians who had kept in touch during peace time with militia service. Clowes was a regular, an artilleryman who led the Anzac Corps artillery in Greece, in 1940. The AIF 18th Brigade was commanded by Brigadier George Wooten who had led the same three battalions in Libya. The two brigades, AIF and militia, numbered 4,500 infantry; there was a battery of the 2/5th Field Regiment and the balance of Army troops numbered about 4,200. Clowes' senior staff officer was Colonel Chilton, a young solicitor who first saw action at Bardia. The General placed the experienced AIF battalions in what he expected to be a second line, ready to counter-attack; the 61st Battalion was spread out in company strength, at Ahioma, KB Mission and around Number 3 strip.

The first sight of enemy movement was made by two coast watchers who reported seven fifty-foot long barges moving along the Papuan north coast, towards Goodenough Island, obviously intending to land on the north Papuan coast to make a flank attack overland on Gili Gili. The following morning, 25th August, aircraft sighted 3 cruisers, 2 transports, 2 tankers and 2 minesweepers heading for the Milne Bay entrance. That night a RAAF tender acting as a scout in the bay – which was continuously overcast with low, squally weather – reported, before midnight, that the enemy force was half-way up the bay. At 1am the foremost sentry near Ahioma challenged several figures moving through the rain and darkness; he was shot and then four Japanese fell as the Australians opened up. As more enemy landed and moved along the track, the Australians moved back, faster when they saw a tank crawling along. When the tank stopped to cross a log bridge, its commander was shot when he stood up in the turret. When night gave way to very dim morning light, the invasion ships were seen to be moving out of the bay to avoid aircraft and the possibility that the defenders were manning guns bigger than their 25-pounders.

When the enemy was first sighted, the RAAF squadron commanders, Jackson and Turnbull, decided to leave the easy barge targets for the time being and concentrate on the invasion ships. Kittyhawks and a couple of Hudsons attacked with guns and bombs – and the convoy kept coming. The fighters had better luck when they flew out to stop the seven barges; they were found beached on Goodenough Island and, after several strafing runs, were all set alight, stranding the troops and destroying their stores. In their next action, Kittyhawks made good strafing strikes on a transport but were unlucky with their bombs which were a new addition to the plane and they had only practised dive-bombing, an impossible tactic through low cloud. B-17 Fortresses came over to lend a hand and they missed too, a sad habit with the Fortresses in those days. (When one sank a Jap destroyer in the Solomons, its captain was furious that he had been so unlucky: 'They always miss!' he said when picked up from the sea, 'Why should it happen to me?') The Hudsons stopped a destroyer which managed to limp away.

On the morning of the landing, the Kittyhawks began a series of strafing attacks which were to continue as often as they could be refuelled and re-armed. In the first raid, accompanied by Hudsons, every barge in sight was sunk or fired with incendiaries, spoiling the ship-to-shore night service and destroying stores. Fuel drums being floated ashore were set alight, as were stores on shore, an ammunition truck was exploded and the edge of the shore was strafed. Zeros flew in from Rabaul, and two of them were quickly shot down by 75 Squadron pilots. The following day eight dive-bombers escorted by twelve Zeros came in to hit the strip and only one dive-bomber escaped; two Zeros were also shot down and one RAAF pilot was lost. In supporting the troops on the ground, the fighters made enormous contributions, machine-gunning until their barrels increased in size from .5-inch to .6-inch. Squadron-Leader Turnbull was killed on one of those strafing runs.

In their second thrust, made at night, the Japanese advanced up to KB Mission. On the way, they captured several natives and bayoneted them after trying their thumbs behind their backs. Thick jungle surrounded most of this village of several huts, situated about one hundred yards up from the beach. The Japanese were supported by tanks that switched on headlights to dazzle and to light up the terrain. An advance patrol from the 2/10th Battalion moved up to help the tired 61st who had been involved in close fighting during the night. When a flame-thrower was used, the Australians hurled grenades at its blinding light and destroyed it. Some Japanese called out in English to retreat – and two platoons did. The enemy armour was still moving along the soggy track when the 2/10th moved up, without anti-tank guns or anti-tank rifles. As their historian reported:

'The men were quiet. . . the silence was broken by a strange sound coming from the east. . . when a light was seen through the jungle an angry voice yelled: "Put out that bloody light." It was then thought to be one of the battalion's light Bren-carriers. They were the headlights of two Jap tanks. Those lights, set deeply in heavy steel reflectors, were each directly beneath a machine-gun. . . the ground ahead was illuminated as by the headlights of a motor car, giving the Jap gunners a very good field of fire along the beam. Moreover, the actual lights and bulbs were so small, so deeply set inside their steel reflectors that only a carefully-aimed shot at very short range and from the very centre of the beam had any hope of putting out the light. . . in trying to

douse them, some of the battalion lost their lives. . . the line was dead and a lieutenant was sent back to request an anti-tank gun. . .'

An eerie prelude ensued before the fighting recommenced at 10 o'clock that night, and soon after the tank's lights were turned on; the quietly-waiting infantry heard high-pitched chanting from the depths of the jungle. 'One voice (and a beautiful voice it was) would recite for about one minute, after which the chant would be taken up by a number of other voices, rather nearer to where the 2/10th lay . . . the second group, obviously comprising some hundreds of the enemy, and closer again, would sing in sonorous unison. This procedure was repeated three times. Whether it was some form of religious rite, or merely a boasting recital calculated to inspire courage in the chanters and despair in the hearts of the listeners is not known, nor did the battalion ever hear again this type of musical performance.'

The airstrips at Milne Bay which were vital to the Allies and Japanese alike

B Company of the 2/10th took the brunt of that night attack by tanks and infantry using rifles, automatic weapons, hand grenades, light mortars and bayonets, everything banging away at a range of twenty yards. Blue, red, green and yellow tracers lit the black night, also brightened by a grass hut set alight in the Australians' sector. B and C companies suffered heavy casualties as the battle intensified, and the Japs suffered more as they tried to move forward, their tanks holding back all the time until the infantry won ground. This was the kind of fighting in which the Japanese had become expert through training and experience; just to be on the edge of it, in the blackness, the rain, the dank stink of the jungle would be confusing enough without the shooting and the menacing tanks with their blazing headlights and withering machine-gun fire. The battalion's historian who was there that night described the problem caused by two tanks:

'As one tank's ammunition grew low, it would withdraw to refuel and be replaced by the other . . . battalion headquarters was well peppered with a noisy but not very dangerous type of light mortar, and some casualties resulted, but here, too, most of the fire passed over, despite the almost point-blank range. Lieutenants Gilhooley and Baird of the artillery party were both killed during the first hour of the fight. Time and time again the Japs attacked B Company, at intervals of a few minutes. Private Jim Kotz took charge of a Bren gun after three men had become wounded whilst serving it. Single-handed he advanced under heavy fire and silenced a post. Later he dashed forward with a grenade and killed three of the enemy who were threatening the company HQ. Although suffering severely from a wound in his chest, he marched back with his company to his own lines. He was to be awarded the Military Medal.

'Several of the enemy parties penetrated the lines, but were promptly despatched with the bayonet, but gallant Lieutenant Scott was killed during one of these attacks. The Japs appear to have little knowledge of how to use the bayonet, and were repeatedly routed by B Company's use of the weapon. The one objective of the enemy obviously was to drive straight down the main track, without any attempt at disguising their intentions, or any finesse in their tactics. These battering-ram tactics persisted for $3\frac{1}{2}$ hours, heavy fire continuing throughout. . . it had become apparent to the enemy tank commanders that the 2/10th had no weapon capable of putting their armour out of action, and they began to grow bolder. . . There were only three sticky grenades per company. From close range they threw them but they did not stick. Sergeant Spencer and also Lieutenant Mackie,

as did others, too, used all their grenades without any effect on the tanks. . .

'The tanks' tactics began to break up the formation on the perimeter, causing some disorder as parties dodged the charging headlights and the bullets streaming down the beams. In the darkness and noise, control was becoming difficult, but through it all the CO was patiently awaiting the long-expected anti-tank gun, knowing that a few well-placed shots would spell the end of the tanks.'

The anti-tank gun, however failed to materialize and the battalion was forced to withdraw. Major Martin was sent back to reconnoitre the line to be held at the rear, but the Japs were outflanking the battalion and he was caught and killed in a short but furious fight by a group of Japs. The fighting passed over and around the battalion. At daybreak, on the 28th, the CO led a large patrol back to the Mission where there were still forty-eight men, including the Company Commander, and a very few Japs who were quickly eliminated.

'The party collected several wounded, among whom was Private A J Abraham, who, although wounded, had spent the night fighting off persistent Jap attempts to get past him. He had received five bullets through his leg and at times lost consciousness, but still clung to his Bren. He was unwittingly left behind when the platoon was withdrawn. A patrol, sent out from the party, found Abraham conscious. Ten Japanese had been attacking him. He had killed six and had four still attacking from behind the cover of a hut. During the night a tank had charged him a number of times but he managed to roll out of danger.' Abraham was awarded a DCM.

During this action which held off the main body of the Japanese for four vital hours, B Company lost 17 killed and 13 wounded, the rest of the battalion 26 killed and 13 wounded. The company took the sting out of the attack which continued against two of the Queensland militia battalions who, in their first blooding, showed the AIF that they could fight like veterans. Before the 2/10th moved back, an anti-tank rifle was brought up – one of those long, heavy Boyes which push the firer back rather than thump him in the shoulder as the 20mm shell is fired. Corporal O'Brien carried it out to an exposed position on the road, lay in the mud, fired at the first tank at a range of ten yards and stopped it. He then aimed at the second tank and, with two shots, stopped it too. Before he withdrew, a Japanese in the second tank stood up and hurled a grenade at O'Brien who was wounded. Another DCM. It took B and C companies two days to extricate themselves from the KB Mission area, withdrawing through the thick jungle and very short of food.

As well as the noise of night battle on land, there were sounds in the bay, of barges and ships, ominous sounds which could mean a second landing on the other side of the bay. To Clowes the danger was obvious and he held on to his reserve battalions, maintaining a narrow base perimeter with the rear clear in case he needed to move back to the hills. During the battle there was little chance for anyone to dry their feet and, seriously for infantrymen, they – and the Japanese – suffered badly from foot infection in the fungus-breeding heat and moisture.

As the 25th Battalion moved up, a truck loaded with sticky bombs, Molotov cocktails and extra ammunition was sent along the road to Rabi, and an anti-tank gun was, at last, sent forward. But alas, the truck bogged down in the road so it was turned into a road block and the Japanese closed in on the gun so it too was disabled and abandoned. Artillery fire had been withheld when their observers were killed and the line to the infantry cut; and it was again withheld when firing indicated that a friendly platoon was in the target area; the platoon cut down about fifty enemy. That was during the night of the 27th. The following day was a day of rest for the troops, for the Japanese were fighting at night and playing possum by day. However, they were not to get the rest they hoped for; Kittyhawks worked them over from daylight to dark, wearing out barrels as they fired thousands of rounds into the scrub where the enemy was thought to be; many rounds

One of 75 Squadron's Kittyhawks takes off to attack Japanese positions

Corporal John Alexander French

were wasted, many found their mark.

Australian commanders were not in the habit of sending out hour by hour reports of battle to base headquarters, particularly when base could do nothing to help. At Milne Bay the enemy owned the sea, coming and going as he pleased and sheltered from air attack by the foul weather. He might bring in a thousand or ten thousand reinforcements and they could land anywhere on some fifty miles of the bay's coast, but, at this hour, what could anyone at base do to help?

That day, the 28th, MacArthur's Chief of Staff, General Sutherland, sent one of the many rude and arrogant signals that were to come from his headquarters: 'The Commander-in-Chief requests that you instruct Major-General Clowes at once to clear the north shore of Milne Bay without delay and that you direct him to submit a report to reach General Headquarters by 8am (29th) of the action taken together with his estimate of the enemy's strength in the area. Please further request General Clowes' opinion as to the possibility that a second movement of enemy shipping into Milne Bay was for the purpose of withdrawing forces previously landed.'

Blamey's deputy, General Vasey, wrote to General Rowell, the New Guinea Commander, who passed on the order to Cyril Clowes. Vasey, already a veteran of two wars, added in his communication to Rowell: 'You possibly do not realise that for GHQ this is their first battle, and they are, therefore, like many others, nervous and dwelling on the receipt of frequent messages. . . I feel that a wrong impression of our troops had already been created in the minds of the great. I am now awaiting the result of Cyril's activities yesterday. I'm dying to go to these buggers and say, "I told you so – we've killed the bloody lot." '

MacArthur believed that all commanders should drive their troops non-stop at the enemy, a continuous never-ending charge regardless of casualties. He seemed to have developed the mantle of the mad imperious generals of the First War who imagined themselves, from the safety of remote headquarters, leading the charge over the top, and carrying on up to Valhalla after a painless, decoration-winning shot through the heart by a sniper. If such people had transferred themselves from imagination into reality, they would have made excellent Japanese privates. Fortunately, the Australian character was against dangerous bravado and foolhardiness, although sometimes some people 'did their lolly' and took on too much, like Corporal French in the action on the 4th September, when Japanese machine-guns were holding up the Australian advance along the track. Corporal French, a tall Queenslander, ordered his section into cover, and with grenades rushed the first of a group of three machine-gun posts. He silenced that gun, returned for more grenades, attacked again and silenced the second gun. Then, firing a Thompson sub machine-gun from his hip, he rushed the third gun, killed its crew, but died himself from wounds, on the edge of the gunpit. He was awarded a Victoria Cross. There were quite a few like Corporal French in New

Major-General C Clowes

Guinea, not all of them recognised with the highest award for valour, some not recognised at all.

The Australian battalion commanders (who had been careful of their men in Libya, Tobruk, Greece and Syria and who preferred to withdraw rather than wantonly waste men's lives in foolhardy do-or-die action) were informed that MacArthur and his HQ staff were dissatisfied with the slowness of the Milne Bay victory and the progress on the Kokoda Track. If MacArthur had come up to the front and expressed these opinions to the men there would have been a general strike. The Japs might have come out in sympathy. Blamey received the complaints and, being a 'good soldier', passed them on.

No matter what the generals wished, it was not possible for troops to fight all night and all day, nor was it possible to fight in any other direction than along the narrow ledge of land that was a morass of mud and a jungle of trees and scrub. This was the time when Blamey should have stood more firmly by his men and insisted on less interference from GHQ in his command of the army. It was too easy for the people at GHQ to run around saying, 'We only want to fight the Japs,' – an expression commonly heard, said Vasey. The Deputy Chief also expressed his opinion that, 'MacArthur's trouble is that all his navy has gone to the Solomons and he wants information on which to base a request, or demand, on Washington to get it back.'

On that score MacArthur had cause to worry, for the operations in the Solomons had escalated, and had drawn heavily on Japanese forces intended for their Milne Bay operations; if they hadn't, the outcome might have been different and the two Australian brigades and all the other troops and airmen might have been forced to retreat. Radio Tokyo had announced that the US Marines on Guadalcanal were like 'summer insects which have dropped into the fire by themselves.' Lieutenant-General Hyakutake, commander of Seventeenth Army in the SWPA also sent more men into 'the fire' and, when the Marines slaughtered a regiment of the 35th Infantry Brigade, its commander, Colonel Ichiki, tore up his regiment's colour, burned the shreds and committed *hara-kiri* (hara: belly, kiri: cut). That defeat was on the 21st August. Hyakutake sent another two divisions, one diverted from New Guinea, into the same Guadalcanal fire, prolonging the battle there until December.

Major Bicks, an Englishman from Twickenham, who was commanding a company of the 61st Battalion, led a daylight patrol to the scene of the previous night's action, saw evidence that when the Japanese had been forced to retreat at Gama river they had shot their own wounded; and saw shot and bayoneted natives, and several Australians whose hands had been tied behind their backs, arms broken by gunshot wounds, and then bayoneted. While Bicks was making his patrol, MacArthur was signalling Washington about the situation, adding: '. . . am not yet convinced of the efficiency of the Australian units and do not attempt to forecast results.'

The defences were now concentrated

near the cleared, unused Number 3 strip, a tempting 5,000-foot long field for a marathon banzai charge. At 3am on the 31st, the Japanese were forming for an approach when flares fired by Australians outlined the enemy for rapid and accurate rifle fire accompanied by streams from machine-guns. Just before dawn three blasts on a bugle recalled the remaining Japs to the jungle. During the night Clowes sent the 2/12th Battalion forward to support the 61st on the strip and also to move around to KB Mission. Apparently dead Japanese were suddenly sitting up and firing, so it was ordered that all prone Japanese were to be shot. They found a native boy and a woman, both horribly mutilated, and two bound and bayoneted Australians. The stories of atrocities hardened the men against taking prisoners, and strengthened their determination to kick the enemy out of Milne Bay. That night militiamen killed 90 of about 300 screaming Japanese who charged out of the jungle. The 2/12th probed forward and the 2/9th was released from the wharf area and joined in the fighting. At one stage Corporal Gordon killed six enemy with his Thompson, one of them after a duel from behind trees at about five yards' range.

At night the Japanese destroyers would race in and fire salvos of shells into the defenders' area, usually without causing many casualties. A wandering Zebu cow was blown up when she trod on a mine near the Air Force canteen where the orderly in charge, believing the Japs to be near-by, destroyed the stocks of beer. He was not quite court-marshalled and shot. The Australians were now on the offensive, not charging wildly into the fire of machine-guns (though a few did), but stealthily skirmishing forward. On the 5th, the 2/9th went in behind an artillery barrage and fighter strafing, the Japanese retreating further until they were forced to give up what remained of their main supply base. The following night,

when the destroyers again entered the bay, they played their searchlights on the supply ship *Anshun* which was unloading at Gili Gili, and sank her with gun fire. The *Manunda*, its hull already illuminated to show its identity, was also illuminated by the enemy twice that night and was not fired on. Clowes expected a fresh attack from another landing, but the Japanese were picking up their defeated men, not sending in reinforcements. They had lost 350 stranded or dead on Goodenough Island, 300 drowned when the RAAF sank a transport in the bay, and 700 in the land fighting. On the morning of the 7th, a cruiser and two corvettes took away 600 wounded and other survivors, the last of the Japanese invasion force.

MacArthur sent a very odd comment to Washington: 'The enemy's defeat at Milne Bay must not be accepted as a measure of relative fighting capacity of the troops involved. The decisive factor was the complete surprise obtained over him by our preliminary concentration of superior forces.' He criticised Clowes' handling of the battle, expecting him to have 'acted with great speed' across the impassable roads, while a second or third landing could have out-flanked him. Blamey gave his official support to MacArthur but Rowell, who was to clash later with Blamey in New Guinea, backed Clowes: '. . . I'm sure that he was right. Inability to move except at a crawl, together with the constant threat of further landings, made it difficult for him to go fast or far.' Politics held Blamey back. He should have told MacArthur where to get off; instead he was to support the man in more hurry-it-regardless-of-costs orders to field commanders who knew how to beat the enemy and how to avoid unnecessary casualties among their own troops, particularly their valuable trained and experienced men.

This was the first complete land victory over Japan since the war began and, minor though the action

A Japanese barge washed up after the abortive landings at Milne Bay

may have been, the news of its success was very heartening – to all Australians at home, to the command who had wondered about the militia, to Marines at Guadalcanal, and to the British in Burma where General Slim's Corps was fighting at Arakan. In his memoirs, *Defeat Into Action,* he wrote: 'If the Australians, in conditions very like ours, had done it, so could we. Some of us may forget that of all the Allies it was the Australian soldiers who first broke the spell of invincibility of the Japanese Army; those of us who were in Burma have cause to remember.'

At the end of this small battle at the eastern corner of New Guinea, Milne Bay was suddenly strategically valuable in a reverse way to that which the Japanese intended; transports and invasion barges would assemble to carry Allied troops, beneath the safe umbrella of Milne Bay-based fighters, to landing beaches near Japan's New Guinea bases. Milne Bay was a nice little victory – for the RAAF too – that in a way balanced the unpleasant news from the Solomons where enemy warships were altogether too successful, and from the Owen Stanley Range where Australians were falling back along the Kokoda Track.

West of Port Moresby, along the south coast of Papua and Dutch New Guinea, only one place was of any great interest to the Japanese: Kokonau, which was about 325 miles north-west along the coast from Merauke. They evidently decided in

1942 that this inhospitable country, edged with vast areas of swamp, was of very little military or commercial value. They were quite wrong, for Merauke was developed, by RAAF signallers, American anti-aircraft gunners, Australian and Dutch infantry and, later, RAAF fighters and dive-bombers, into a worthwhile base. Japanese aircraft occasionally raided the airfield and seaborne patrols came out from Kokonau in 1943 to seek the outposts developed by the Australians. A minor naval engagement took place on 22nd December when two forty-foot long Japanese barges, carrying ten Japanese approached within machine-gun and mortar battle distance of a launch transporting Captain Wolfe and a party of engineers on a survey mission. The Australians replied with Bren and rifle fire and, as the vessels closed, with grenades. After two minutes of shooting and throwing, the enemy withdrew. As a result of this encounter a post was established near the mouth of the Eilanden river and was manned with machine-gunners who were on duty when the enemy returned, as expected. This time they were in three barges and five launches but they never made the shore, losing about sixty men when the Australians opened fire. RAAF aircraft and army patrols were in control of this section of the southern New Guinea coast for the duration of the war.

65

Kokoda Track

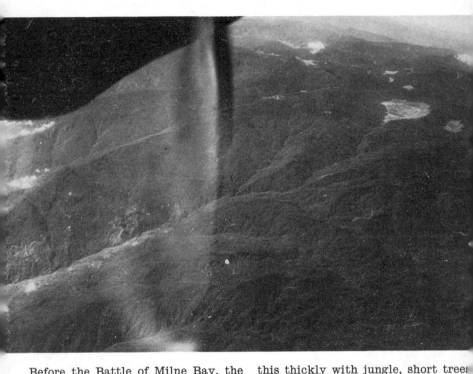

Before the Battle of Milne Bay, the campaign in New Guinea had already begun on two vague fronts: in the Markham Valley where the hopelessly outnumbered commandos and New Guinea militia riflemen were fighting a guerilla war, and along the Kokoda Track. Colonel Kingsley Norris, 7th Division ADMS, described the country: 'Imagine an area of approximately one-hundred miles long. Crumple and fold this into a series of ridges, each rising higher and higher until 7,000 feet is reached, then declining in ridges to 3,000 feet. Cover this thickly with jungle, short trees and tall trees, tangled with great entwining savage vines. Through an oppression of this density cut a native track . . .' That was the Owen Stanley Range over which the Track ran and through which fighting was to take place for the immediate protection of Port Moresby. There was a road from the Port, just twenty-five miles of it to Uberi, on a plateau in front of the main range; from Uberi the track rose 1,200 feet in the first three miles, part of it up the 'Golden Staircase'. The steps of the stairs varied from ten to

eighteen inches in height, the front
edge of each step was a small log held
by stakes and behind each log was a
puddle of mud and water; some of the
logs had worked loose and tilted so
that anyone tripping on them fell
back into mud or against trees or
banged his head on his slung rifle. To
help their legs and to prevent falls,
the troops cut long walking sticks. It
was the weight of the 45-pound pack
and a rifle – or a Bren gun – that made
it more difficult, although an unladen
soldier quickly tired after the first
dozen steps and then, as a 2/14th

Left: **The terrain through which the
Kokoda Track is cut.** *Above:* **The
problems of fighting, bringing up
supplies and evacuating the wounded**

Battalion soldier said, 'it became a
matter of sheer determination forcing
the body to achieve the impossible.
The rear companies, where the going
is always hardest, took twelve hours
to complete the nine miles,' – barely
four miles as the crow flies.

After climbing 1,200 feet, the track
dropped 1,600 feet before the final
climb of 2,000 feet up the Imita range –

almost vertical in the last few hundred yards. The days were humid and hot, the nights bitterly cold, and the rain almost continuous, which made, reported a 2/16th man, 'the track a treacherous mass of moving mud interlaced with protruding roots that reached out hidden hands to bring the laden troops heavily to the ground. Vines trapped them. Wet boughs slapped at them. Their breath came in gulps. Their eyes filled with perspiration.' There were mosquitoes, mites, chiggers and leeches, and malaria, dengue fever, dysentery and jungle rot, making healthy men emaciated and gaunt. As they marched the increasing heat of the day produced a steam from their permanently wet clothes. After Imita there were more ranges before the centre ridge at Myola, then the track followed a ledge down to Templeton's Crossing at Eora Creek, then up and down again for about ten miles to Kokoda, half-way to Buna, which had been an administrative centre, and Gona, an old mission. From Kokoda to Buna – about forty air miles – the country was not quite as rough and there was more downhill than uphill for men marching north.

Before Brigadier Porter sent forward his 39th Battalion (militia, reinforced with some AIF officers and NCOs) he gathered large teams of native carriers to be their supply column. General Morris of Angau had invoked National Security Regulations to conscript native labour that was normally available for plantation labour or carrying, but they were not very anxious to be forced into work. When more troops went into the range there were never enough native carriers to bring up supplies of rations, ammunition, weapons, and other equipment which were always insufficient or delayed. The natives' crinkly hair inspired the Diggers to call them 'fuzzy-wuzzies' and generally they had a cheerful regard for each other. Sometimes the natives were overworked and overloaded, times that

were critical in saving the country from occupation and a grim future of 'Co-Prosperity' for the Melanesians. Plantation horses, mules and wild brumbies (horses) caught in the Bootless Inlet area were also used to pack supplies along parts of the track. They had to carry their own fodder and the natives, too, were partly loaded with their own supplies; a carrier carrying only foodstuffs consumed his load in thirteen days so to man-carry food on the eight-day journey to Kokoda meant that the supply system would soon break down without drops from aircraft. The Japanese, though their rations were lighter, were also to learn the bitter facts of basic logistic requirements in this country where there was a shortage of local foodstuffs. The rich soil, rainfall and climate grew excellent vegetables and fruits, but the native gardens were cultivated for a limited supply only: there was never a need to lay in big stocks, productivity being so reliable.

Optimistically, Porter's 30th Brigade was to advance all the way to Buna-Gona with AIF troops following, and behind them a corps of two American divisions commanded by Major-General Robert L Eichelberger. To begin with, MacArthur's plan included securing the crest of the Owen Stanleys from Kokoda to Wau. The Allies were beaten to the punch. On 21st July, Japanese cruisers and destroyers escorted transports to Buna and, the following day, to Gona. Fortress and Mitchell bombers attacked and the results were too typical of the USAAF bombing standards at that time to do much damage to the enemy at sea or on the beaches. The landing was the reason why the militia battalion was hurried out to block an enemy advance on Kokoda. Brigadier-General C A Willoughby, MacArthur's chief intelligence officer, suffered under the fond delusion that the Japanese had no intention of marching overland to Port Moresby, even after the Coral Sea battle and after the Milne Bay landing. He believed that the enemy

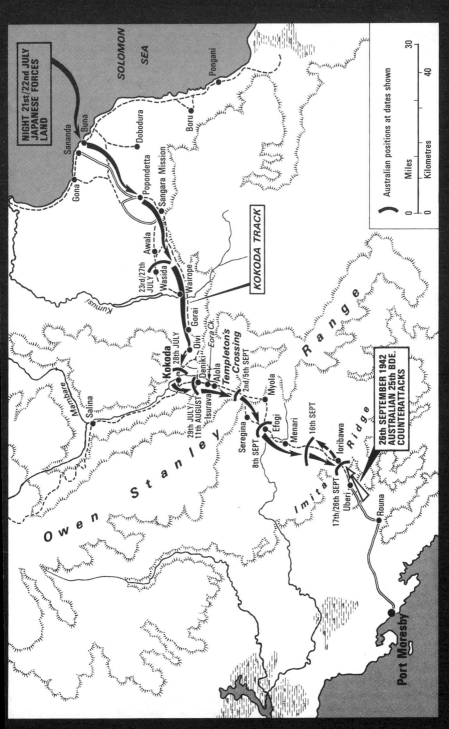

The Kokoda Track; the overland offensive against Buna

Above: Native carriers who brought up the supplies for the defence of Uberi and the attack on Kokoda. *Below:* Lieutenant-General Robert L Eichelberger and General Sir Thomas Blamey. *Right:* Australian and Papuan troops with native carriers

The mud of the Kokoda Track which the Allies fought over to capture Buna

wanted possession of the Gona-Buna-Kokoda area to establish airfields from which to raid Port Moresby and Allied bases in North Queensland. He was to persist in this view for many months, allowing it to influence his estimates of Japanese strength and, as a result, causing him to consistently underrate the Japanese forces in numbers as well as quality. From this staff officer, MacArthur received information which probably inspired him to think that when the Australians were driven back along the track, they were retreating before a numerically inferior enemy force. Another glaring example of stupidity among the C-in-C's staff was the recommendation by his Chief Engineer to block a certain pass, called the Gap, by demolition; even if there had been a narrow trail passing between towering rock walls there was no reason why anyone would not be able to clamber over rubble left by demolition.

Such errors led one Australian junior, though experienced, staff officer to think that GHQ had been taken over by a bunch of crackpots who did not understand the qualities of Australian troops, the strategic needs of the enemy, or the terrain where the campaign was being fought and that, until they had a war where they would have unlimited mechanised transport so they could 'git thar the fustest with the mostest' (the axiom of Confederate General Nathan Bedford Forrest), they would be floundering in impatience, suspicion and nervousness.

A battalion of Papuan Light Infantry at Buna retreated when the 2,000 Japanese landed, and on the way back along the track most of the native infantrymen 'went bush' so that when an advance company of the 39th arrived in the Kokoda area they were too few to hold the airfield. Kokoda was some six miles from the main track which branched at Deniki, a place developed into a defence position. Further back, at Myola, was the bed of a dry lake, a saucer in the mountains, and this became a suitable area for air drops, then quite primitive in technique. Stores were dropped in double sacks to ensure that at least most of the contents were not lost. From Myola, the supplies were carried to dumps at Templeton's Crossing. Eora Creek, Alola and Isurava by Angau's natives, overworked and for a time on very short rations. As pressure from the Japanese increased, it looked as though supplies so far forward would not be needed for very long.

When the under-strength battalion finally went into action, it was in small patrolling groups setting ambushes and skirmishing. Anyone wounded and left behind or captured at this time was never heard of again. The 39th attempted to gain ground against advancing Japs who lost the greater number in the process but who, nevertheless, forced the Australians to fall back. At Kokoda on 9th August the Japanese vanguard was held, and an officer wrote in his diary: '. . . the enemy's fire forced us to withdraw. The platoon was scattered and it was impossible to repeat our charge . . . The night attack ended in failure. No. 1 Platoon also carried out an attack about 0300 but it was unsuccessful. Every day I am losing my men. I could not repress tears of bitterness. Rested waiting for tomorrow, and struggled against cold and hunger.' The following evening the Japanese chanted from their positions and one called out in English, 'You don't fancy that, do you?' 'Never heard worse,' replied an Australian before the Japanese launched their attack. After an hour and a half, the enemy had suffered heavy casualties but were still numerous. The Australians withdrew. At Deniki, the enemy 'came up the hill four or five abreast, in shorts and helmets . . . Lieutenant Simonson's

platoon beat them back with grenades and Tommy-guns,' in the rain and mist. Compared with the large frontal assaults which were to occur later in New Guinea, these were very minor yet important in that they delayed the enemy, and time was of the utmost importance to the Allied programme. The fighting here was to develop in pockets near the track so that there would never be any massive build-up on what might loosely be described as the front line.

The delaying actions were stronger when the 53rd Battalion moved up to help the 39th (the AIF called them 'those ragged, bloody heroes') who had borne the brunt for about three weeks. Their CO, Lieutenant-Colonel Honner, wrote: 'Physically the pathetically young warriors of the 39th were in poor shape. Worn out by strenuous fighting and exhausting movement, and weakened by lack of food and shelter, many had literally come to a standstill. Practically every day torrential rains fell all through the afternoon and night, cascading into weapon pits and soaking the clothes they wore – the only clothes they had. In these they shivered through the long chill vigil of the lonely nights when they were required to stand awake and alert but still and silent...' Extracts from on-the-spot reports give a truer picture of the situations than statements issued from GHQ where the defeated general from the Philippines was asking for victories. It was, in fact, remarkable that the untried militia were facing up to these conditions and close contact with the enemy, who were, as Dudley McCarthy accurately describes in *South-West Pacific Area – First Year*, 'brave and strong of purpose . . . hard and enduring... not tied by their own supply lines. When they met the opposition they felt for the flanks and then spread to move round and envelop it before they tried to move over it. In attacking prepared positions they came back again and again to the same point – although they might switch tem-

Above: 'Fuzzy Wuzzy Angels', bring back a wounded American soldier while
(*below*) Australian troops carry a wounded comrade on a makeshift stretcher
Right: Curious natives around a US transport plane

porarily – trying to create a weakness through which they could break. They followed any withdrawal so closely that their opponents found it difficult to make a clean break and to retain the initiative in patrolling. They used the high ground off the tracks to great advantage. They used camouflage well. Their weapons and equipment were light, their communications good. They adapted local devices and conditions to their own use.'

They were the best that Hyatutake could muster for General Horii and they had had experience in either China, the Philippines or Malaya. Originally, there were the 124th and the 41st Infantry Regiment groups, an engineer regiment and two artillery regiments as well as service troops. The Second Infantry Group were sent to Milne Bay, but Horii still had about 13,500 troops with him when the advance into the Owen Stanleys gathered momentum.

On the other side of the mountains, the AIF 7th Division, less the brigade which had gone to Milne Bay, were tramping up the 'golden stairs' on their way to assist the militia battalions. The 21st Brigade, led by the 2/14th Battalion, arrived when the enemy attacks had become heavier and persistent enough to be continuous. Battle-weary men moved behind the brigade which was learning the tricks of jungle fighting. Commanding points were established with machineguns as the dominant factor, both sides became expert at setting booby traps along the jungle paths, and sniping and ambushing were everyday events. The Australian chain of command now was: Major-General 'Tubby' Allen – who had commanded a brigade in Libya, Greece and Syria – had the Division; he reported to General Rowell of New Guinea Force HQ; he reported to Blamey, and Blamey reported to MacArthur. At GHQ, General Vasey heard and passed on reports from either end, and added personal messages of his own.

US troops cross Eora Creek on their way to Kokoda and Buna

Even if it had not been forced on them, it would have been a good idea for the Australians to retire back to the ranges near Moresby, to shorten their supply and reinforcement lines and thus lengthen the enemy's. The Japs had no air transport fleet, whereas the Allies were building one, and Allied fighters were too dangerous for Japanese bombers to do much supply dropping. On 1st September, Horii received another 1,000 fresh troops which he sent up to reinforce the 124th Regiment. General Allen had no intention of wasting his troops in the the same quantities that Horii lost his, and as Allen became familiar with the situation, he was formulating a plan for a prolonged counter-offensive, when the time was ripe. The 2/14th and 2/16th took over Jap-killing withdrawal movements from militiamen who were still in action in early September. In one of their first actions, on 29th August, the 2/14th were under a fierce attack that was driven off by a counter-attack in which Private B S Kingsbury won a Victoria Cross, awarded posthumously, for clearing a path through the enemy with his Bren fired from his hip. That day the enemy lost about 200 men. Sections, platoons and companies were fighting the war: there was no room for larger formations. If the supply position had improved for the Australians, the fighting might have continued in this area around Eora Creek; as it was, the supply system was collapsing. There were shortages of the most essential items – such as green camouflage uniforms, and trenching tools instead of the bayonets, helmets and empty tins they were using to dig fox-holes. Wounded men walked back and if they couldn't walk they were carried on stretchers by natives – 'fuzzy-wuzzy angels' – and some wounded supported each other as they walked and sometimes crawled back. From Eora Creek back to

Templeton's Crossing stretcher bearers tramped for about six hours; from the crossing to Myola took up to twelve hours and a climb of 1,000 feet. The general condition of wounds in these circumstances was however good, owing to the extensive use of sulphanilamide, placed on the wound and taken orally. 300 carriers were used to bring wounded back from the crossing to Myola where, after a six-day rearguard action, the two AIF battalions were forced to make a short stand before retreating further.

The Japanese were driven hard by their officers to try to get ahead of the Australians and keep up pressure on their flanks. There were continuous clashes from which the Australians usually managed to extricate themselves with few casualties, though sometimes they were heavy. One such occasion was on the 8th when a company of the 2/27th lost six Brens in a dawn attack and retaliated by using up 1,200 hand grenades and thousands of rounds of ammunition until the enemy withdrew. The AIF brigade were learning all the jungle survival lore while they retreated back to where HQ in Moresby suggested should be the last stand: Ioribaiwa, a few hours' march and about eight miles from Uberi. This was close enough to Moresby to get reserves and stores up quickly, and far enough from Buna to strain the supply situation for the Japanese. Neither Allen nor Rowell had any doubt, now, or at any time, that they could keep the enemy from capturing Moresby by an assault from the north.

Early that month Vasey wrote to Rowell: 'GHQ is like a bloody barometer in a cyclone – up and down every two minutes . . . they're like the militia – they need to be blooded.' Their dissatisfaction with the slowness of the Milne Bay victory influenced their views about the Kokoda Track and it seemed that MacArthur and his American staff had no idea of the true position. On the 6th September, he advised Washington: 'The Australians have proved themselves unable to match the enemy in jungle fighting. Aggressive leadership is lacking.' Vasey had to forward on a similar message to Rowell and neither of these men could understand Mac-Arthur's attitude. The troops were standing up to it at least as well as MacArthur's force did in the Philippines retreat and, because they weren't being driven to foolhardiness by arrogant generals, their morale was high. Just learning the jungle trade took time and experience, as Alan Dawes points out in *Soldier Superb:*

'Jungle genius is an infinite capacity for taking pains. It is an acquired resiliency to the thousand blows man and Nature can inflict in the miasmic stronghold of tooth and claw. It is the faculty to fight on when your head is awhirl with malaria, when your bones are cracking with dengue, when your belly is pinched with the hard, hot kunai grass, or your boots waterlogged, your clothes soaked with sweat and ooze in the mountains of mud; when fear is in the trembling of a leaf and not mercy but murder rains from heaven; when nothing is what it seems but a trick by a cat-cunning enemy. Jungle genius is above all the power not to conquer these terrors, but to tame them to your will and your need and enlist them as allies, use them as artillery against your enemies.' One day MacArthur would have huge forces going on the offensive against Japanese troops, his men would be well fed, properly clothed and equipped, given the comforts of PX stores, and backed by colossal fire power and reserves. The fighting in the Owen Stanleys was a divisional commander's war, on a narrow front where tactics were dictated by local conditions and events. Because it was a slow slogging match, MacArthur and his staff thought that there must be a lack of dash and fire in the Australian camp and he worried the generals to inspire some.

A fresh 7th Division brigade, the

25th, arrived dressed in their new jungle greens to join the fighting at Ioribaiwa, close enough to Moresby for friend and foe to hear the sounds of aircraft on the strips. Morale in the Japanese lines was as high as ever, higher perhaps because they were so close to their goal; morale in the Australians' lines was also high, especially when the brigade of AIF marched up. Horii maintained his tempo of attack and Brigadier Eather was forced to move his 25th Brigade back to Imita Ridge. General Allen told him on the telephone, 'There won't be any withdrawal from the Imita position. You'll die there if necessary. You understand?' Yes, Eather understood. Others were also bringing pressure to bear. MacArthur told Prime Minister Curtin that the Australian troops were inefficient, when only a few hours before the Prime Minister had agreed with Rowell's opinion that the enemy could not take Moresby from the Australians. MacArthur worried Curtin by saying that the Australians were withdrawing while the Japanese weren't, and they, he said, were weaker in numbers. So, when MacArthur asked for Blamey to go to New Guinea and take over the show, Curtin agreed to tell him to go. This was a delicate situation for Blamey who hoped to be able to operate in New Guinea without interfering with Rowell's work. He wrote to the New Guinea commander explaining the situation, adding, '. . . we have very inexperienced politicians who are inclined to panic on every possible occasion, and I think the relationship between us personally is such that we can make the arrangement work without any difficulty.' However, Rowell could not see how he could operate with a superior on the scene and a split between them formed and widened. At the end of September Blamey relieved him of his command and sent for Lieutenant-General Herring to replace him.

While this result of MacArthur's trouble-stirring chat with the Prime Minister was developing, the campaign proceeded along the lines planned by Rowell, Allen and the brigadiers, in a style which the fighting troops knew so much better than any generals. And, on 12th September, the advance party of Brigadier-General Hanford McNider's 126th Infantry Regiment of the 32nd US Division arrived at Moresby. Two brigades of the AIF 6th Division – which had been held at Churchill's request in Ceylon while on their way back from the Middle East – had returned to Australia and prepared for service in New Guinea. The third brigade had arrived direct and gone to the Darwin area. At Ceylon, the 16th and 17th Brigades had gained some tropical training but, as Rowell pointed out, reinforcements should be trained to master the difficulties of tactics, movement and control in New Guinea jungle country. Queensland, and even dry-wet Moresby were not typical enough of the country where they would be going into action. Rowell also emphasised that in jungle and mountain warfare, wastage of personnel from battle casualties and physical exhaustion was very high, and this meant that it was essential to have reserves of fresh units as well as greater infantry numbers generally. MacArthur adopted Rowell's idea and sent a force on a pioneering trek across Papua, well away from the Kokoda Track, to attack the enemy from the rear. The US Regiment was chosen for this operation.

Back at the Ridge both sides took a breather. On the 19th a strong patrol located a Japanese post being fortified; it was knocked out in a grenade, sub machine-gun and bayonet charge. A few more were added to Horii's casualty list which was now about 1,000 dead and 1,500 wounded. Australian casualties were 314 killed and 367 wounded. Whenever the Australians overran an enemy post there was little evidence of food. About half a pint of rice per day was the Japanese official allocation – if they could get it across from

Buna. When they attacked and took Iorabaiwa they headed hungrily for the Australian supply dumps which they had noted in their recces, and were disappointed to find the supplies had been carried away. If they had bean paste they could make soup, otherwise they ate native garden produce – as did the coast watchers or anyone stationed near villages – potatoes, lotus bulbs, pawpaws, bananas and pumpkin. In some areas tomatoes could be picked a few weeks after throwing an old tomato onto the rich soil. Short-sightedly, the enemy did not establish large vegetable gardens when he sent many thousands more troops into New Guinea.

Imita Ridge stopped them; the sound defence position, the strength of the patrols, the two 'short' 25-pounders dragged up the 'golden stairs', the growing superiority of Allied aircraft, and mounting Japanese casualties from disease and hunger. From now on the Australians were prepared for an offensive; they had fresh troops and their supplies were building up satisfactorily at Moresby – which would have been lost if the militia brigade had not done so well, and was almost lost again through the tardiness of GHQ in moving up the AIF. Now that they were going on the offensive they could have sorted out the logistics for the long trek ahead: they had the lesson before them of a Japanese withdrawal through lack of supplies, and it was time to bring up more air transport – including adapted bombers and more civilian aircraft than they had already commandeered. Fit men, sick men and the wounded required more nurturing in this country because of the climatic conditions. If there had been sufficient bearers all the time it would not have been so bad, but most of the time there was a shortage of native labour. In some steep parts of the track, eight men were required to carry a wounded man who would suffer painful jolts or be spilled out of the stretcher. When men were cut off they could starve.

Sergeant Irwin of the 2/14th used his watch as a compass to lead his platoon, cut off and lost in the mountains; they took twenty-two days, nineteen without food, to work their way back across ravines and jungle ridges. Some took days to return, others were missing for weeks. One man, wounded in the ankle, was cut off with several others who offered to carry him on their backs or on a stretcher. He refused and crawled for three weeks, in the heat then the cold, soaked and mud-caked, starved and exhausted. When they reached a native village the man, Corporal Metson, was left in a hut with other wounded. Tragically, they were found by Japanese who killed them all. These reports of experiences of hardship were accumulating at headquarters and the picture of conditions was becoming clearer to the planners.

It was easy for people to be cut off in that wild jungle country. One company of the 2/27th that had been sent wide to reconnoitre at Menari was delayed, having to hack a track through vines and thick scrub, and then were cut off during the retreat. The CO, Captain Sims, described his experience, typical of many from that company:

'We had our first meal when we shot a pig in a village on the 14th September . . . troops had dysentery and were very weak from hunger . . . burnt pig meat on our bayonets . . . two other groups came in . . . ate everything . . . shot a cockatoo and every bit was eaten including the bones. I had pneumonia and tropical ulcers. By the time I got back I had dengue too. Every man in the company lost 2½ to 3 stone . . . met patrols from the 2/14th and 2/16th cut off at Templeton's Crossing and Myola . . . Whoever could go on without calling a halt would get ahead.'

The majority of the 2/27th had also been cut off and they were still straggling back in October, having suffered severely in the mountains; yet their losses were lighter than would be expected: 41 dead and 46 wounded, the rest weak from malnutrition and disease. The experiences of the 2/27th stretcher parties and their wounded are stories of selflessness, gallantry and endurance.

The 25th Brigade led the way north from Imita Ridge back along the Kokoda Track, wider now that it had been used by so many of both sides. Other advances were being made and Kanga Force was slowly gathering strength in the Markham area. Within ten days the brigade were back at Eora Creek and Templeton's Crossing and were already feeling the pinch from lack of supplies. Air drops were being made but they were not often or heavy enough. There were not enough carriers and when the troops went into the front line – or where the front line might be – they were burdened thus, as the official history states:

'Each man carried up to five days'

rations (2 days' hard and 3 emergency), half a blanket, a groundsheet, soap, toothbrush, half a towel, half a dixie, a water-bottle, his weapon and ammunition. One shaving kit was usually carried for three men. Within each battalion each rifleman carried his own rifle and 100–150 rounds of ammunition; one 3-inch mortar with fifteen bombs was carried by natives when these were available, at other times by the mortar crew assisted by HQ company men and sometimes by men of the rifle companies; one Vickers machine-gun, with two or three belts of ammunition, carried similarly to the mortar; one Bren per section carried in turns by each member of the section with ten magazines per gun distributed among members of the section; 2 sub machine-guns per section carried by gunners with 5 magazines and 150 loose rounds; one 2-inch mortar to each platoon carried by mortar members with 12 rounds distributed; 2 grenades carried by each man. Each battalion had five

A Japanese bunker effectively silenced by Australian troops near Buna

carrier loads of medical gear; cooking gear; two picks, two axes; one machete and one spade per section; six telephones and six wireless sets. The Japanese equipment was lighter though their bellies were emptier. Some were eating the flesh from killed Australians.'

MacArthur wanted Kokoda captured as quickly as possible, so that the force could be built up by airlifting men and supplies to its airfield. Blamey urged General Allen to 'press the enemy with vigour. If you are feeling strain personally relief will be arranged . . .' Allen quickly replied: 'The most serious opposition to advance is terrain . . . This country is much tougher than any previous theatre, and cannot be appreciated until seen . . . Am not feeling the strain. I have never felt fitter, nor able to think straighter. I, however, feel somewhat disappointed on behalf of all ranks that you are dissatisfied with the very fine effort they have made . . .'

The drive continued against such obstacles as dense bamboo where Japanese in one-man pits could only be attacked with grenades, high positions which required crawling uphill attacks, heavy machine-guns dug into concealed positions, and that awful Japanese speciality – sniping. Unless a battalion or brigade commander wanted to lose men unnecessarily, he could only probe carefully, reconnoitre cautiously and move slowly along the main track. Diverging for flanking movements was rarely possible because of the terrain and blocking jungle. On the morning of 17th October the militia 3rd Battalion, attached to the AIF brigade, fought their way into a strong enemy position and captured much of their equipment. Captain Atkinson described a sniping duel that morning: 'When Richardson was shot, Downes, a country lad, with his pipe in his mouth, tried to spot the sniper. I went down to bandage Richardson (who was breathing through a hole in his chest). A bullet went between my pack and my back and hit my dixie. Downes saw the muzzle blast, moved out into the open to see better, and shot the sniper. Then he calmly went back behind a tree, took his pipe from his mouth, turned round to the boys and said, "Well, I got the bastard!"' We had one stretcher bearer, Dwight, and he used to go out whenever anyone was hit and would go where others wouldn't go. He got one man out of a forward pit, going under fire for some yards, lifting him, putting him on his back, and then running 150 yards under fire.' There was no medal for Dwight, who was killed in action the following month, and none for numerous men whose acts of bravery went beyond the call of duty. Also on the 17th, Allen called up Brigadier Lloyd's 16th Brigade, which Allen had commanded in Libya, Greece and Syria.

'Along the route,' recorded the 16th Brigade, 'were skeletons picked clean by ants and other insects, and in the dark recesses of the forest came to our nostrils the stench of the dead, hastily buried, or perhaps not buried at all.' The battalions – 2/1st, 2/2nd and 2/3rd – were the first of the AIF to go into battle during the war – at Bardia in December, 1940. Now, nearly two years later, after having fought Italians, Germans and Vichy French, they were to test themselves against the Japanese. It was platoons and companies moving on the narrow front against enemy pockets defended with mortars, machine-guns, grenades and rifles. The actions were to be repeated over and over again on the track and in fighting right across the New Guinea fields of battle: a battalion, brigade, division and reserves strung out behind a small group of men in the forward points; men falling under fire, the enemy pinpointed and a sergeant or corporal leading a few men into the ridiculous gamble.

It had to happen and it happened time and again. 'He swung left then across to Baylis's feature where he brought his depleted force in behind the other company as support. By that time the other forward platoon commander, Blain, was dead, with a number of his men, and Barnes, leader of the third platoon, was wounded . . . As Goodman's first section moved down it was pinned by machine-gun fire. The other two sections swung out of the fixed lines. Corporal Roberts closed his section on to a machine-gun post and bombed it into silence. The Australians kept pressing against the remaining strength of this position, able to see little in the thick bush . . . after the attackers had followed on for about another 150 yards heavy fire smashed into them again and held them close to earth . . .' These are a few of the many scenes at the fighting near Eora Creek, the valley below the climb up to the Kokoda plateau. At night, the dead from both sides lay in grotesque positions, and the rain fell, persistent and cold; the Japanese could be heard chattering and moving about.

If the Japanese did not open up to disclose their position so that an attack could be made and one more unit of enemy aggression wiped out, then a scout would be sent forward to trigger off an enemy reaction. That was the way the war was being fought in this awful campaign, and the troops fought superbly because they were a self-contained group, with excellent morale and confidence, and not because GHQ or NGHQ or Divisional HQ were itching for progress.

Lieutenant B H MacDougal, one of the original members of the 2/3rd Battalion had this to say about the scouts when interviewed by a Sydney newspaper: 'On the march . . . each leading company had to send scouts out ahead on the track. It was almost a certainty that once a day, or perhaps more often, the forward scouts on the track, or scouts exploring the Japanese positions across the track would be killed or wounded by unseen snipers, who would wait until they were twenty yards away or less before firing. Yet there was never any diffi-

culty in finding men for the job. Before the leading platoon moved off in the morning or after a spell, the commander might say, "We'll need two forward scouts." Three or four men would begin to collect their gear and come forward. These three or four would arrange among themselves who would to out in front. One would say to another, "You did it yesterday," and there would be some quiet discussion until, in a few seconds without any more orders or suggestions from the platoon commander or sergeant, two scouts would be selected and ready.' That kind of battalion spirit only shows itself among veterans and when the battalion had grown into what might be called a brotherhood – certainly a kind of family – the men hated to leave it and they would fight to return after recovering from wounds or illness, or refuse promotion if it meant transferring to another unit. Against such battalions the Japanese had no hope whatsoever of getting to Moresby, or of staying in New Guinea.

From the Creek they fought uphill against a series of prepared positions beyond which were strong main defences with a long perimeter. It turned out to be the main defence of Kokoda and the fighting for the Eora Creek stronghold lasted until the end of the month. The cost to the 16th Brigade was ninety-two dead and about 200 wounded. If there had been more time perhaps the casualties would have been lighter. Allen had been pressured from GHQ: on the 17th came a classic MacArthur signal, one that belonged to the Crimea generation of generals. 'Press General Allen's advance. His extremely light casualties indicate no serious effort yet made to displace enemy. It is essential that the Kokoda airfield be taken.' Blamey tried to show the sense of Allen's actions by explaining in a signal the next day that 'his difficulties are very great. In addition to the terrain and the constant rain, supply-dropping grounds are very

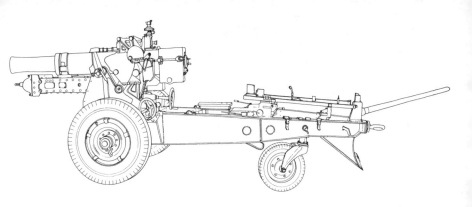

The short 25-pounder gun/howitzer was a special development of the standard 25-pounder to suit it to the generally appalling conditions of the New Guinea campaign, where light weight and manoeuvrability were of paramount importance. Details for the standard model. *Weight of shell:* 25-lbs (20-lbs armour piercing). *Range:* 12,500 yards (13,400 yards with super charge). *Rate of fire:* four rounds per minute. *Crew:* six men

few, and recoveries are not as great as one would hope.' The next signal which MacArthur sent to Blamey was passed on to Allen, and its text considerably hurt the 7th Division commander: 'Operational reports show that progress on the Trail is not satisfactory. The tactical handling of our troops, in my opinion, is faulty. With forces superior to the enemy we are bringing to bear in actual combat only a small fraction of available strength, enabling the enemy at the point of actual contact to oppose us with apparently comparable forces. Every extra day of delay complicates the problem and will probably result ultimately in greater casualties than a decisive stroke made in full force. Our supply situation and the condition of the troops certainly compares favourably with those of the enemy, and weather conditions are neutral.' MacArthur seemed to believe that there was just one compact Japanese force immediately in front of Allen against which he should throw his whole division.

MacArthur continued to pressure Blamey and Blamey continued to urge Allen to press harder. Against lighter opposition the Japanese had taken fifty-one days to advance from Kokoda to Ioribaiwa in their drive to Port Moresby. It had taken the Australians only thirty-five days to retake the same distance of track, fighting an enemy more experienced in jungle fighting than the 16th Brigade, an enemy who had an intimate knowledge of every yard of the narrow front, and who fought with much less regard for human life. Impatiently, MacArthur waited for the inevitable move – Blamey's dismissal of Allen. The signal was sent on 27th October: 'Consider that you have had sufficiently prolonged tour of duty in forward area. General Vasey will arrive Myola by air morning 28 October. On arrival you will hand over command to him and return to Port Moresby for tour of duty in this area.' Allen was disappointed that he could not stay, now that the worst was over, and wait until his troops could also be relieved. Five days later Kokoda village was re-entered according to plan, an inevitable event whether the division had a general or not.

Buna, Gona, Sanananda

In one of his signals to Allen, Blamey had said, 'You must realise time is now of great importance. 128 US already has elements at Pongani. Capture Kokoda aerodrome and onward move to cooperate with 128 before Buna is vital portion of plan.' The 128th Regiment, and the 126th, were the infantry of Major-General Edwin E Harding's 32nd Division; they were National Guardsmen, the equivalent of Australia's militia, and had been recruited two years before in Michigan and Wisconsin. They were not terribly well trained, as Lieu-tenant-General Eichelberger dis-covered when he arrived in August to take over the American Corps. Never-theless Harding was confident in the fighting qualities of his men and thought that when they were sent against Buna 'we might find it easy pickings . . . may be a bum guess, but even if it proves to be incorrect I do not think it would be too much to take Buna with the forces we can put against it.' He was sadly misled. He thought the Japanese were aban-doning instead of reinforcing Buna and another American observer sug-

gested that GHQ was 'afraid to turn the Americans loose and let them capture Buna because it would be a blow to the prestige of the Australians who had fought the long hard battle all through the Owen Stanley Mountains, and who therefore should be the ones to capture Buna.' The American involvement with prestige emanated from GHQ, and existed, with jealous intenseness, between MacArthur and the other Pacific Commander-in-Chief, Admiral Nimitz.

The flanking movement against Buna from the south was a sound

Opposite: **The Australian flag is raised over captured Kokoda.** *Above:* **A 'flying-fox' is used to cross the Kumusi River**

move. A group of Americans were flown in to prepare an airstrip at Pongani about forty miles down the coast from Buna; the 128th Regiment flew to Wanigela to join the AIF 2/10th Battalion flown in from Milne Bay; a combat team from the 126th marched across country, parallel with the Kokoda Track, and, when the rest of the regiment flew in to Pongani, they

Lieutenant-General Hatazo Adachi

moved to Bofu. The AIF 2/6th Independent Company (commandos) also landed at Wanigela and, while they marched to Pongani, the 128th moved around by boat and together the Australians and Americans pushed forward along the coast to Oro Bay. By the middle of November the plan was set: the US division (with a detachment of AIF artillery and the commandos) was to advance on the Oro Bay – Bofu line south of Buna, which was to be their objective; the Australians would advance on two other fronts – 25th Brigade against Gona and the 16th Brigade against Sanananda.

To get to their objectives the Australians first had to finish their advance across the Track. When their grenades, bullets and bayonets had won Kokoda, there was quite a celebration, especially among the natives who wore flowers in their fuzzy heads and more readily volunteered for carrier work. They had accepted Japanese domination as they had for years accepted German, then Australian; but they had come to realise that the Japanese were the worst masters, who raped and murdered and forced carriers to work until they dropped. In the Markham Valley there

were many, notably native police, who remained loyal to the old administration. At Kokoda, an old police 'boy' came in from the bush wearing nothing but his old battered cap, and rushed up to the first Australian he saw, exclaiming, 'Hey! Japan 'e sorry too much now!' Yet there were others, including village heads, who had great influence over their people, who spied for the enemy.

Horii, his white horse dead in a mountain valley, was certainly suffering as he withdrew his troops. His retreat was hampered by the destruction of the wire bridge over the deep river valley at Wairope (pidgin for 'wire rope'). Defeated units moved back behind prepared defences all the way, giving both Australian brigades difficult and costly work in clearing Oivi, Gorari and other points on the way to Wairope. In two days the Australians lost forty-nine killed, 123 wounded, and the enemy lost 150 killed. The following day the enemy lost over one hundred while the Australian losses were very light during attack and counter-attack. In one action, a Japanese officer swung his sword at the head of an Australian who had emptied his gun and was changing the magazine; the sword cut the man's helmet from his head and when they grappled he kneed the Japanese and was 'twisting him down with his hands' when another Australian shot the swordsman. With the bridge down, the Japanese were forced to abandon much of their stores and equipment, dumping them into the river. Horii joined some of his troops escaping on rafts downstream to Lae and was drowned when his raft capsized in the rapids. Others escaping to the rough mountain country, and some of the survivors on rafts, were shot by patrolling Papuan infantrymen. Japanese losses for that week were probably as many as 1,000. The Australians built a suspension footbridge across the Kumusi river where battalions of heavily laden troops and long native carrier lines gathered to

Major-General Edwin F Harding

make the crossing, either over the bridge or by a high-strung 'flying fox'. This point was in the foothills of the mountains and virtually the end of the Kokoda Track; the end of the Battle.

At least 6,000 Japanese front line troops fought in this part of the New Guinea campaign which cost Australia 625 dead and 835 wounded. Also, thirteen were killed and nineteen wounded when the 2/12th Battalion from Milne Bay landed to mop up Goodenough Island and secure the passage for transports to bring around supplies to the new Allied landings on the New Guinea coast.

That November, Lieutenant-General Imamura took over the responsibility of the Solomons and New Guinea operations; his Eighteenth Army in New Guinea was commanded by Lieutenant-General Adachi whose headquarters were established at Rabaul. There had been two defeats – at Milne Bay and on the Kokoda Track – yet Imamura still believed that he could win the campaign and take Port Moresby. For the Kokoda-Buna-Gona operations, about 18,000 army and navy troops were involved – including reinforcements, the III/229th Battalion, marines of the 5th

Yokosuka and 5th *Sasebo*, and engineers, gunners and service troops who had either just arrived or had not suffered the rigours of the Track. Construction troops were employed in digging and strengthening defence positions and, while the ground positions were fortified, Adachi could not provide an air cover to match the Allies. He was still able to get supplies through by ship from Rabaul, a line that had little chance of survival as Allied air power increased in numbers and, at last, hitting power. While he could land and establish bases across the top of New Guinea he was, although he obviously did not accept the idea, contained by Allied arms and air power from Buna to Lae. Hyakutake's Seventeenth Army in the Solomons was fully committed against US Marines, in the air and on land, and the naval battles in that area were swinging in favour of the Allies. Midway had destroyed Japan's hope of retaining mastery of the oceans and this meant that if the New Guinea and Solomons campaigns were lost, there was little chance of them being relieved with massive help from other Japanese sources.

Supplies and air power were two factors which now favoured the Allies, a different situation from that of a few months back. Zero fighters from the 'Lae Wing' were restricted to the coastal area and were not allowed to fly over the Owen Stanleys to pick fights with their enemy. The Buna-Gona area as well as their own base suffered constant attack from Allied fighters and bombers, a situation that called for patrols and interceptions over Lae, Salamaua, and the supply beaches. The Allies had only one RAAF Kittyhawk squadron doing any worthwhile work at the beginning of the campaign; by 1943 General Kenny's Fifth Air Force and the RAAF were hammering away with scores of B-25 Mitchell bombers, P-40, P-38 and P-39 fighters, Boston bombers and Beaufighters, taking the war to Japan's southern Pacific possessions.

Opposite: Australian troops bridge-building on the Kokoda Track to Buna
Above: An American patrol 'feels out' the enemy in preparation for the final attack on Buna

During 1943 they would gain such superiority it would be dangerous, whether on the ground or in the air, for the Japanese aircraft to be seen.

American infantry approached Buna along the coastal road, inland through Dobodura where engineers cleared a landing strip, and further inland to approach between Gona and Buna. Much of the country in between was swamp, some of it tidal, and the rest kunai grass and scrub. 1/128th and 111/128th battalions went forward to attack the coastal plantation of Duropa and were thrown back in confusion by machine-gun and rifle fire. Americans and Australians had been ordered by MacArthur to drive through to objectives regardless of loss. The Australians weren't that silly, and General Harding did not whip his men to suicide. There was

delay getting Colonel McCoy's American battalion into action and, after they did move, some retreated back and had to be gathered by their officers. Australian commandos led an attack for another battalion, but while they moved forward, clearing several machine-gun posts and knocking down snipers, they were forced to halt because the Americans hadn't moved. Another battalion fell back when Japanese troops broke up an inexpert approach. A decade later, Eichelberger wrote his after-thoughts of this poor beginning:

'The 32nd Division, like the Australian militia, was unprepared for the miseries and terrors of jungle warfare, and in both forces some of the men failed . . . Actually, this long after, I'm inclined to believe that the men were more frightened of the jungle. It was the terror of the new and the unknown. There is nothing pleasant about sinking into a foul-smelling bog up to your knees. There is nothing pleasant about lying in a slit-trench half-submerged, while a tropical rain turns it into a river. Jungle noises were strong to Americans – and in the hot moist darkness the rustling of small animals in the bush was easily interpreted as the stealthy approach of the enemy.'

Old soldiers, apparently, can take anything – as the AIF demonstrated and also the Americans once they, too, had some experience behind them. But at that time, November 1942, the 32nd Division was causing grave concern. General Kenney noted that stories of inaction and even cowardice were filtering back; officers did not know their jobs and commands were too far to the rear; if they waited long enough the Japs might starve to death or quit; every day there were planeloads of shell-shocked and sick boys being sent back; there were cases of men throwing away their machineguns in panic, and their officers did not know what to do. Plans were made to send up more Australian artillery and tanks which were arriving at Milne Bay, but there was no barge big enough to bring up a tank so arrangements were made to send up a platoon of Bren carriers, useless in swampy country. Bombing and strafing did not dislodge the enemy from his fox-holes and bunkers, and the flat swamp and kunai country afforded the gunners no observation for effective shooting with 25-pounders and 4.5-inch howitzers. The position improved when RAAF advanced trainers, two-seater Wirraways, were brought up to act as spotter aircraft for the guns; they noted shell bursts, discovered enemy ack-ack positions when they were fired upon. While a few were shot down to crash in flames, the planes generally performed a duty that was essential to assist the Americans. One Wirraway actually shot down a Zero.

Ammunition was brought up at night to the guns in canvas assault boats dragged for two miles along the surf from the dump. Shells and cases were then carried for about a mile through the dark jungle. The Americans were facing fresh, well-fed and well-armed troops dug in behind log barriers while they themselves were suffering from swollen feet, short rations, exhaustion and malaria. The enemy was expert in camouflaging the walled and roofed log emplacements with screened loopholes, emplacements which withstood gun and mortar fire, and stopped the Americans. MacArthur decided to relieve Harding and summoned Eichelberger.

To the Commander of I US Corps, MacArthur said, 'I am sending you in, Bob, and I want you to remove all officers who won't fight. Relieve regimental and battalion commanders; if necessary, put sergeants in charge of battalions and corporals in charge of companies – anyone who will fight. Time is of the essence; the Japs may land reinforcements any night . . . I want you to take Buna, or not come back alive.' The following morning he added enticement to threat: 'If you capture Buna, I'll give you a Distinguished Service Cross and recommend you for a high British decoration. Also, I'll release your name for newspaper publication.' This kind of encouragement would have shocked Australian commanders who felt that the American system of publicising individuals did not help military operations and could create bad feelings. Blamey, who resented any personal publicity for himself, could see no reason why one officer should be limelighted over another. Australian decorations were never promised, only given – and then in comparatively small numbers. MacArthur was sensitive in matters concerning what should be added to his beribboned chest and was quite steamed up when Curtin suggested awarding him with the same decoration – Knight Commander of the Order of the Bath – that was offered to General Brett. A fracture in their friendship was avoided by the Prime Minister getting a higher award for the C-in-C – Knight Grand Cross of that order.

Eichelberger stopped his troops'

activities for two days while he sorted out the positions of units which were too scrambled for Harding to explain. Harding was replaced by General Waldron and the attack was renewed on 5th December, with mortar, artillery and air support for the infantry's frontal assault on Buna. Five AIF Bren-gun carriers, open-topped and lightly armoured, were towed up in a barge and went into action, manned by experienced Diggers. Too vulnerable – to sniper fire from tree positions, to lobbed mortar bombs, and straddling over big logs – the carriers were all immobilised. They had thrown out some withering fire while they were mobile, spearheading the III Battalion attack. The same kind of fire was returned, halting the battalion. There were gains in the 1/128th's sector where individuals were showing up as determined fighters, knocking out the enemy and holding on. Remembering his orders, Eichelberger was right up with them, encouraging his men, as he has de-

scribed in *Jungle Road to Tokyo*: 'My little group and I left the observation post and moved through one company that was bogged down. I spoke to the troops as we walked along. "Lads, come along with us." And they did. In the same fashion we were able to lead several units against the bunkers at Buna village.' When the Division's third regiment, the 127th, arrived fresh from Moresby on 9th December, they began to relieve the II/126th who had been successfully resisting Japanese counter attacks from the Government Station. So far American casualties amounted to 667, including 113 killed, and another 1,260 were sick. The AIF 18th Brigade and some tanks from Milne Bay were, at last, embarked and on their way to lend their weight to the assault on Buna.

The AIF brigades which had come down from Kokoda also suffered from shortage of food supplies, malaria and

Australian and American troops arrive at a typical jungle landing field

not enough rest – the now normal aftermath of anything from one or more weeks campaigning in the jungle. 16th Brigade went forward through swamp, bush and kunai grass towards Sanananda, running into accurate artillery fire directed from tree observation posts, and intense small arms fire. The brigade had suffered heavily on the Track, its numbers were reduced and most of the troops were ill. It was a matter of honour among them that no-one reported sick unless his temperature was over 103 degrees; one man walked a couple of miles to the RAP where he said to the MO: 'I don't feel so hot, doc.' But he was – 106 degrees. Nevertheless their fighting spirit was as strong, or more so, than ever. When a group from the 2/1st Battalion, ten officers and eighty men, made a recce and discovered the position of the gun that was causing a lot of damage, they attacked against main enemy positions without their own battalion support, for they were out of communication. They crept up to within fifty yards of the enemy before being spotted, then charged into their midst, killing eighty in the first assault. They lost five highly experienced officers and a large number of men killed and wounded. There was no chance of getting the wounded back and the fight continued for two days and two nights until they were relieved by a company from 2/3rd.

When the American 126th Regiment first arrived to relieve the brigade, they were fortunate in having another troop of 25-pounders supporting them when they went into action. The 126th were not successful and their careless aiming of mortars killed veteran Australian officers and some of their own officers and men. With the 16th Brigade depleted – having lost 605 killed and wounded, and hundreds through sickness – and the 126th too inexperienced, another reserve was brought up: 30th Brigade of militia, bolstered with AIF officers and NCO's. The militiamen were at least fresh

and one company, of the 49th Battalion, gained 800 yards while losing all platoon commanders and fifty-eight of the company's original ninety-eight. In December the situation was that the Japs were still in their well-concealed strongpoints and the three Allied brigades were baffled. Relief for the 16th was long overdue. They were now down to fifty officers and 288 men; the 2/2nd Battalion was only about one hundred strong, or weak, for they could hardly carry their automatic weapons. The Americans were not keen on taking the offensive and the other militia battalion, the 55/53rd, were prone to go to ground too quickly. Opposing them, in mid-December, were 6,000 Japanese, including sick and wounded, and about 1,300 fresh troops who had been brought in from Rabaul by destroyers. Sanananda was the strongest of the three enemy positions. While it and Buna were besieged, Gona was attacked by the AIF 25th Brigade.

As this depleted brigade, aided by a company from the 2/14th and the 3rd battalions, came in from the scrub and swamps, they were met by a tenancious defence in kunai clearings. Stalk and consolidate tactics were used against a defence of trench systems, slit trenches and gun posts which had a wide creek on the western perimeter. Within two weeks the brigade had lost 204 killed and the usual high proportion of wounded and sick. A day of bombing gave them a respite and quietened the Japs without wrecking the strong log emplacements – the formidable obstacles which the Allies were to find everywhere in the Pacific. Also formidable was the tenacity of the enemy who would fight to the death in these stinking holes, starving, diseased and with their dead rotting and unburied beside them. The obstacles were a different problem from those faced during the guerilla fights in the mountains, a problem Vasey and his commanders either had to solve or leave the enemy contained behind

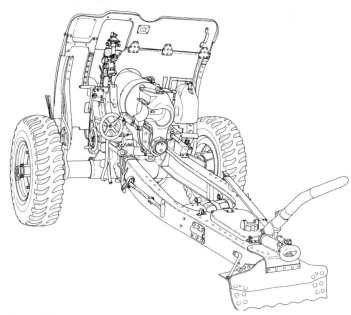

The British 4.5-inch howitzer. Barrel length: 13.33 calibres. Weight of shell: 35lbs. Maximum range: about 7,000 yards. Elevation: −5 to +45 degrees. Weight of gun and carriage: about 3,000lbs.

large, permanent patrols. Perhaps that would have been a better plan.

When Brigadier Ivan Dougherty, an ex-6th Division battalion commander, led a refreshed, reinforced 21st Brigade down to Gona, he decided that one of the three enemy bases should be taken first instead of the three being attacked at the same time; the loss of Gona would weaken Sanananda and its loss would weaken Buna. But how? His militia brigade and the under-strength 2/14th Battalion – the group that had done so well delaying the enemy approach to Moresby – were to move on the right flank to the beach and fight in from there, while 25th Brigade worked at the front and a battalion stood on the western bank of the creek. They fought hard and desperately to get into their positions, the 2/14th doing the hardest work and making possible the cut through to the beach, thereby getting between Gona and Sanananda. On 1st December, Dougherty launched his major assault behind a barrage of artillery

and mortar bombardment, an assault which failed, at great cost, to penetrate far enough. Within five days the brigade suffered 340 casualties and were forced to pull out. The gunners now had delayed-action fuses for their shells which could explode about two feet underground or bore lethally into the log-roofed emplacements before bursting. The guns concentrated again for an attack, this time by remnants of the 2/14th, 2/16th and the 2/27th – in total numbers less than one battalion – plus a fresh 39th. The latter led, following so close behind the creeping barrage, they were among the enemy while they were still recovering from shock. The battle raged all day, reducing the Japanese hold to one small area with a narrow swampy corridor to the beach – where escaping Japs were shot as they tried to get to the sea. Next day, mopping up through the shambles was a nightmare of fighting near the bodies of dead Japs and Australians. 'Gona's gone,' signalled Dougherty, and sent

Opposite: Major-General Wootten and Major Denniston plan to take Sanananda
Above: Australian mortar crews operating less than 200 yards from Gona
Below: Australian troops only thirty yards from Japanese positions

two battalions four miles westward up the beach to knock out, again expensively, an enemy position at Haddy's village. The crocodiles that usually lived in the swamps and swam in the sea, had stayed in the sea; now that the battle was over they were returning to the swamps.

Again the problem of supplies: 'Except at Sanananda, the Jap front is not more than half a mile from the coast anywhere, but he is covered on his front by the filthiest country imaginable and by extraordinarily strong forces . . . our supply has to be taken in by aeroplane . . . landing grounds sometimes out of action because of weather conditions . . . strips not strong enough to take fighter aircraft . . . as soon as our own protective umbrella returns, the news is flashed from Buna to Lae and the enemy comes out on strafing and bombing expeditions . . . difficulty in getting guns across and maintaining the ammunition supply up to them.' That was one of Blamey's main problems; the other was the need for more experienced troops and he pressed the government to demand the return of the 9th Division from the Middle East. In his letter to the Prime Minister, he summed up the situation:

'I had hoped that our strategical plans would have been crowned with complete and rapid success in the tactical field. It was completely successful strategically in as much as we brought an American Division on to Buna and an Australian Division on to Gona simultaneously, But in the tactical field after the magnificent advance through the. most difficult area, the Owen Stanley Range, it is a very sorry story.

'It has revealed the fact that the American troops cannot be classified as attack troops. They are definitely not equal to the Australian militia, and from the moment they met opposition sat down and have hardly gone forward a yard. The action, too, has revealed a very alarming state of weakness in their staff system and in their war psychology. General MacArthur has relieved the Divisional Commander and has called up General Eichelberger the Corps Commander, and sent him over to take charge. He informs me that he proposes to relieve both the regimental commanders, the equivalent of our brigade commanders, and five out of six of the battalion commanders; and this in the face of the enemy. I am afraid now that the bulk of the fighting will fall on our troops in spite of the greatly larger numbers of the 32nd US Division.

'The brigades that went over the mountain track are now so depleted that they are being withdrawn and I am utilizing the only remaining AIF brigade in Port Moresby and a brigade of Militia, that has been intensively trained here, and I think we will pull if off all right.

'The Americans say that the other division which they left in Australia is a much better one than the one they have here, but since they chose this as number one, I believe their view to be merely wishful thinking. I feel quite sure in my own mind that the American forces, which have been expanded even more rapidly than our own were in the first years of the war, will not attain any high standard of training or war spirit for very many month to come.

'This may appear to be a digression from the main subject, but it brings me to the point that in replacement of the 9th Australian Division we have been given two American Divisions, and as their fighting qualities are so low, I do not think they are a very considerable contribution to the defence of Australia. Of course, the American authorities will not admit this but will continue their attitude of wishful thinking. You will therefore see that if the 9th Australian Division is not returned for our future operations in this area we are going

Colonel Murray, General Herring and General Vasey at the Sanananda Front, February 1943

to be in a very bad way indeed. In fact I feel that our position will be definitely one involving considerable risk and danger.

'The 6th and 7th Australian Divisions after the Buna operations are completed must have a prolonged rest out of action. They both have a very large number of reinforcements to absorb and a very large number of sick to return. This means that the defence of Papua will rest for a time mainly on Militia and American forces. My faith in the Militia is growing, but my faith in the Americans has sunk to zero. If the 9th Australian Division is not returned I fear very greatly that we will have to sit down for a very long time in this area in an endeavour to defend it, mainly by keeping the Jap flotillas away by air action.'

The victors of Milne Bay were next brought up and made their presence felt east of Buna. They had with them four tanks – American M3 General Stuarts mounting 37mm guns and .30 Brownings – which could only move properly on cleared, firm ground. The 2/9th started near the hulk of one of the carriers knocked out earlier in the month, and with the tanks and 25-pounders hammering away at the log-emplacements the battalion advanced, a 'spectacular and dramatic assault', commented Eichelberger, pleased to see the Aussie veterans stroll forward. At one post the enemy had captured a Bren and some grenades from the old Bren carriers: 'One of the grenades burst almost in Corporal Thomas' face as he dashed for the post, but, blood pouring from his face, he plunged on and killed two of the Japanese. A third fired at him with a Bren . . . seizing the muzzle Thomas wrestled for its possession and then dragged it through the opening and killed its previous user with it.' The tanks made all the difference while they were mobile, knocking holes in emplacements and protecting infantrymen who protected them when Japs tried to climb onto

Opposite: Keeping weapons dry,
Australian troops advance on Buna
Above: Allied tank engaging Japanese
strong-points in the battle for Buna

them to fire through the vision slits.
Japs tried to light a roasting fire
under one tank, straddled on a log,
but it was saved by accurate shooting
from another tank. In six days the
2/9th had won about a mile of coastal
strip, and in another six days the
2/10th and Americans captured an old
airstrip and were moving towards
Giropa Point. One night there was an
unfortunate incident when American
PT boats, operating from Milne Bay,
set a supply barge alight and fired into
the troops.

Daylight attacks by the Allied
troops, nocturnal counter attacks by
the enemy, accurate shooting by the
25-pounder gunners, pounding by aircraft and shooting by mobile tank-
forts during another fortnight of fight-

ing ended with the destruction of the
thousand-strong Japanese force east
of Giropa Point, about a mile from
Buna where American infantry were
assaulting from the south. Those men
fought on through Christmas, the
front lines as confused as the movement of the enemy and their own
companies. Some were amazingly re-
solute, others inclined to ignore a
soldier's duty to press on regardless.
One lieutenant had to be arrested and
sent back under guard because he was
running to the rear, followed by his
whole company. This whole sector was
very complex, where the enemy could
appear seemingly from nowhere. On
the 29th, a quartermaster sergeant
from the 2/10th led a party of men
carrying rations and ammunition to a
forward company and were resting
near an American casualty clearing
station when some Japanese attacked,
killing or wounding everyone. Those
left alive, including the CQMS, feigned

Curtiss P-40 Kittyhawk 1 *Engine:* Allison V-1710 inline, 1,150hp. *Armament:* six .5-inch Browning machine guns. *Speed:* 354mph at 15,000 feet. *Climb rate:* 2,050 feet per minute. *Ceiling:* 29,000 feet. *Range:* 700 miles. *Weight empty/loaded:* 6,350/9,100 lbs. *Span:* 37 feet 4 inches. *Length:* 31 feet 2 inches

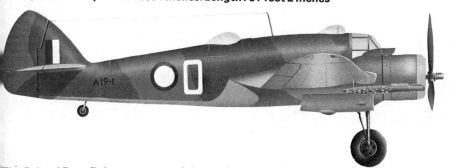

The Bristol Beaufighter was one of the war's outstanding aircraft, and few made a better name for themselves than the Mark IC's operated by the RAAF as the A19. The type was used as a two-seat day and night long range fighter. *Engines:* two Bristol Hercules XI radials, 1,400hp each. *Armament:* four 20mm Hispano cannon and six .303-inch Browning machine guns. *Speed:* 321mph at 15,800 feet. *Climb rate:* 1,960 feet per minute at sea level. *Ceiling:* 26,500 feet. *Range:* 1,170 miles. *Weight empty/loaded:* 13,800/21,000 lbs. *Span:* 57 feet 10 inches. *Length:* 41 feet 4 inches.

death; he kept one hand covering his wrist watch in case a Jap saw it and discovered him still living when he tried to take the watch. Private A B McDonald of C Company, one of the wounded at the CCS, had shot several Japs before he was bayoneted and left for dead. Another patient, Private Joe Leonard, who was ill with fever, was also bayoneted and, in the early hours of the morning, recovered sufficiently to be able to discern a few Japanese on lookout in the kunai grass nearby. From his lying position he threw a grenade which killed or badly wounded every one of them. The CQMS and both privates survived.

In the swamp country which surrounded the area were large crocodiles that occasionally waddled down for a breakfast of fish in the sea. There were small fish that jumped out of the water to bask in the sun on branches of the mangroves, and large green frogs that croaked all night. Incidence of malaria was almost one hundred per cent. At Sanananda the swamp and jungle were typhus-ridden; the swamp was tidal and could swell higher when wind whipped up the sea

Left: Always alert, American troops mop up around Sanananda

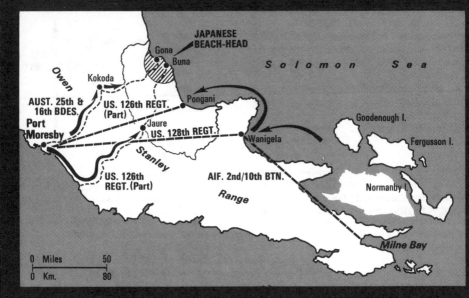

Australian and US forces assemble for the attack on Buna

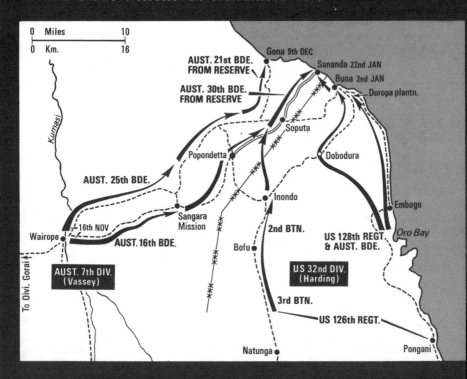

The Japanese are finally evicted from the Buna area

and pressed its waves inland. From the walls of green jungle foliage, crawling roots reached out into stagnant pools infested with mosquitoes and numerous crawling insects. Patrols were made through swamp up to men's waists and higher; the rain came in thunderstorms accompanied by vivid flashes of lightning, and every foxhole filled with water. Thompson sub machine-guns jammed with the gritty mud and were unreliable in the humid atmosphere though Brens and Lee Enfield rifles stood up to the conditions remarkably well.

Early in January the American division, the AIF brigade, a commando company, the tanks and the gunners, supported by fighters and bombers, broke the enemy defence and took Buna. There were 2,900 casualties among the Allies while the enemy lost about 2,000 killed, including two commanders who suicided.

Along the coast at Sanananda there were another 2,000 enemy front line troops to be dealt with in the same agonising way – by frontal attack. Brigadier Porter was given the task and he mustered – apart from service troops, mortarmen and signallers – the 49th and 55/53rd militia (527 altogether), 2/3rd Battalion (119 sick and exhausted) and the 126th US Regiment (545 weakened with sickness and fatigue). To these were added 2/7th Cavalry Regiment (battalion-size and now trained as infantry) and the 36th Battalion, a fresh militia unit. As the fighting progressed, other weary troops were brought into the action which continued until near the end of January. The Japanese fought as they always fought – right to the bitter end; they were almost starving, each man down to a ration of a handful of rice a day to which some added roots, grass and pieces of dead friends and enemies. Along the Sanananda Track they lost 1,600 killed. About 1,000 escaped overland to the west of Gona, and 1,200 sick and wounded were taken off by sea. Some 600 Australians and 70 Americans were killed; their wounded numbered more than 2,000.

Blamey had seen enough of this fighting to form this opinion which he later told Herring: 'I think it is a great error in tactics to hammer away at pockets, since it delays the operation, and leads to a great many casualties. If the pocket is sufficiently covered, I think you should push on to your objective. We can either deal with pockets by starving them out or blowing them out later.'

Australian and American troops developed a liking and respect for each other, fighting and dying together at Buna-Sanananda. They were happy with the alliance although there were some senior officers who were awkwardly blind to the good qualities of their partners. The important thing was that the enmity which had grown between the troops in Australia, particularly at Brisbane, changed to comradeship when they shared the common experience of battle. The ill-feeling in Brisbane had come to a head on the night of 26th November. American MP's killed and wounded eight Australian militiamen during a clash outside a Post Exchange, and the following night, small groups of Diggers roamed the streets, beating up MP's and attacking other American troops and officers. It was called the Battle of Brisbane and was generated by several factors: drunkenness; difference in rates of pay; favouring of Americans in shops and hotels and by taxi drivers; girls and wives of absent soldiers going out with Americans and their custom of caressing in public; American boasting and their tendency to draw knives or guns in a quarrel; taunting of militiamen by Americans; and the display of firearms and batons by MP's and their tendency to use them in an emergency – a factor which might quell Americans but could start a riot among Australians.

Fighting together, they got along famously; apart, they were both too much inclined to 'take the mickey' out of each other and that inevitably led to trouble.

Wau

The middle of 1942 was the darkest period of the war for the Allies – when the Axis powers were all-conquering. The Germans were thrusting the Russians back, Tobruk had fallen and Egypt was threatened, U-boats were winning the battle of the Atlantic and the Japanese were firmly established in South-East Asia. In the first few months of 1943, the position began to change as intense productivity of war material gave the Allies the arms and equipment for their trained multitudes to go on the offensive. At last, overall plans could be made for ulti-mate victory, for which a broad outline was described at the Casablanca Conference in January. The defeat of Germany was the prime consideration, satisfying the desires of Churchill, Roosevelt and Stalin; pressure was to be maintained against Japan – Rabaul was to be taken, advances in the Central Pacific were to be made through the Gilberts, Marshalls, and Marianas; and Burma was to be recaptured. Planning the use of 'adequate forces' – the Casablanca gesture – a Pacific Military Conference in Washington in March allocated

duties to Admiral Nimitz, who remained Chief of the Central Pacific area, and to General MacArthur, Chief of the South-West and South Pacific, with Admiral Halsey his naval tactical controller. With his vow 'I shall return' perhaps influencing too much his future grand plans, MacArthur proposed two lines of approach to Rabaul, then island-hopping and enveloping back to the Philippines and on to Japan. Nimitz preferred a more direct route from the central Pacific to bases closer to the enemy's homeland. Their differences of opinion

Opposite: The ever-present threat of Japanese air attack; a blasted Wirraway
Above: Vital supplies come up for Kanga Force near Wau

meant that there could be no unified command under one Supremo, so the Joint Chiefs of Staff compromised by sanctioning the dual arrangement.

For their 'Operation Cartwheel' in the South and South-West Pacific, MacArthur and Halsey chose points in the Solomons, and islands between them and New Guinea, as suitable for amphibious operations. The land

No reinforcements for Lae get through;

forces in New Guinea would move along the coast to capture the Lae-Salamaua-Finschhafen-Madang area and move into western New Guinea; then the Halmaheras would be occupied so that air bases could be established within striking distance of the Philippines. MacArthur left the New Guinea land forces under Blamey's command but the operational control of Americans making the landings on New Britain and Rabaul would be entirely American. His GHQ would still make the strategic decisions, and keep urging, for a long while to come.

Japan's defeat on Guadalcanal was complete on the night of 1st-2nd February when the remnants, some 13,000, of Seventeenth Army were evacuated in destroyers to Buin and Rabaul. Japan also lost an air fleet of over 600 planes and their crews – most of their experienced, irreplaceable airmen – and lost heavily at sea. Reinforc-

ing Lae, Salamaua and the Markham valley area was now of prime importance. About 2,000 Japanese had been evacuated there from Buna-Gona before the assault and about 3,400 had escaped by boat or on foot, including General Yamamata who got away in a landing craft too heavily laden for safety and speed – until he had some of the wounded and exhausted men thrown overboard. The 51st Division, which had been brought down from French Indo-China to Rabaul, were sent on to Lae, the advance echelon arriving in early January. While Japanese marines were losing heavily in skirmishes with Australian commandos, a strong force was sent to destroy coast watchers and assist the weak and straggling mob coming up from Buna-Gona. The immediate objective was to capture the Wau up-and-downhill airfield as a stepping-stone for another inland approach to Port Moresby.

The small Kanga Force in the Wau-Salamaua-Lae area had not been seriously hunted by the enemy during the operations south-west along the coast; instead, they were rather neglected while the Allies were bent on that offensive. Scanty supplies were sent on a long route from Moresby: first in an old island trading schooner from the port to the mouth of the Lakekamu river, then by native dug-out canoes which were lashed together in catamaran pairs to provide a cargo platform, each paddled through the crocodile-infested waters upstream to Bulldog Camp; from there long lines of carriers (600 were employed altogether) carried the supplies 120 miles over jungle-clad mountains and valleys to the lower slopes and hills, covered with kunai grass, at Wau. The forward base of the 2/5th Independent Company was a reed-thatched hut in a small clearing surrounded by tall trees and thick undergrowth, near Japanese-held Mubo in no-man's land between Lae and Salamaua. NGVR scouts manned a tree observation post overlooking the Japanese in Salamaua and radio messages regarding their movements were sent daily to HQ. Damien Parer, the famous war photographer, visited this area and filmed Japanese planes taking off and alighting in the bay, and Japanese troops less than a mile from his cover.

Coast watchers and Angau men were noticing a change in the natives' attitudes; they were not as helpful as they had been because they were cowed by the Japanese. The fact that Allied planes were continually bombing and strafing in the area kept some wavering loyalties tied to their old 'master' When they changed loyalties they maintained a stubborn, embarrassed silence, so that men on patrols were always in doubt about the presence or absence of enemy soldiers. In 1942 the natives would have instantly informed on the slightest move by an enemy patrol towards an Australian position; in 1943 some of the heads of villages went to the other extreme and simply did not mention enemy movement at all, particularly the surveys being made into the ranges north of the Markham, an area which could be an inland escape route from Lae to Madang – or for a flanking attack from there over to the Markham. While the watchers and scouts could maintain supplies of trade goods, notably salt and razor blades, they were able to live off the land and sustain the loyalties of enough people to hold back the populace generally from total affiliation with the Japanese. Unfortunately, men in the bush were now too often betrayed, falling to Japanese bullets or execution swords.

Mubo, fifteen miles from Salamaua, was about twenty direct miles from Wau – much further along either of the two main connecting tracks – and Fleay (promoted to Lieutenant-Colonel) believed that when the enemy entered Mubo they would press on in usual Japanese style to take Wau. So he ordered 'scorched-earth' action: most of Wau's buildings went up in flames, bridges were blown up and some installations and facilities in the Bulolo valley were destroyed. These precautions proved to be unnecessary, as it happened, but were sound policy at the time. On 4th October another commando unit, 2/7th Independent, was flown up to Wau to reinforce the old hands whose morale remained exceedingly high in the face of their isolation, dangerous situation, constant diet of canned bully beef, disease and discomfort. With the fresh company of 290 men, some of his fitter 2/5th, and 400 carriers, Fleay made a long jungle trek to hit the enemy at Mubo before they hit him. They were moderately successful in that they killed a lot of Japanese while losing only a few of their own men. They returned to Wau to find the 17th Brigade moving in and Fleay's enlarged Kanga Force came under the command of Brigadier Moten, another Middle East veteran. The 2/6th Battalion was first up from Milne Bay, via Moresby, followed by 2/5th and some engineers.

In January, the Japanese began

their move towards the Wau airfield, their main force travelling along a little known jungle track while the Australians were deployed along the two main routes. By the end of the month, 5th, 6th and 7th battalions were fully committed to heavy fighting and their reserve companies, delayed at Moresby, were rushed up. A dawn attack to win the airfield on the 30th was repulsed, with accurate fire cutting a swathe through enemy ranks. The arrival of two 25-pounders, landing at 9.15am from DC-3 Dakotas which were barely missed by enemy shelling, gave the defenders valuable support when they began firing at 11.30am. That afternoon three to four hundred Japanese appeared on a road under the noses of a 2/5th company, led by Major 'Luger Joe' Walker, who were in a perfect ambush position. Supported by 25-pounders and RAAF Beaufighters, the 2/5th opened up with rifles and machine-guns, killing or wounding more than half of the attackers. RAAF and USAAF assistance in the form of transport and bombing and strafing missions played an important part in the defence of Wau airfield throughout the action. Eventually the enemy closed in to a tighter perimeter and the opposing infantry fighting became more intense.

Light mortars, heavy mortars and Vickers machine-guns were the defenders' strongest killing weapons beyond a hundred yards; closer, the fight was with rifles, sub machine-guns and grenades. When Beaufighters could be accurately directed onto Japanese under thick cover, the planes' enormous fire power of 20mm cannon lethally penetrated – as did the 25-pounder shells directed by observers posted in trees or flying in the back seats of Wirraways. A Wirraway and a Dakota were destroyed by an enemy fighter and bomber attack on the 6th February; Allied fighters intercepted and shot down two bombers and thirteen Zeros, anti-aircraft gunners got another bomber and two Zeros.

The battalions were attacking all the time, sometimes killing scores of enemy for few of their own, at other times losing heavily in the numerous small pockets of action. Within a few days, the enemy was retreating from the Wau Valley, where he had suffered a serious defeat, harassed all the way back to Mubo by company patrols and strafing aircraft.

Lieutenant-General Ivan MacKay, then commanding New Guinea Force, was still worried about Japan's numerical superiority in New Guinea and asked for additions to his 11,400 Australians and 8,400 Americans. He advised Blamey: 'Enemy defeats at Guadalcanal and Papua and his anxiety for Lae make another attack on Wau a possibility. Persistent reports from Angau and native agents that the enemy is constantly moving troops overland from Madang via Nadzab to Lae with object attacking Wau most probably via Nadzab, Wampit Valley, Bulwa. Estimate enemy strength Lae-Salamaua 8,000 Madang 5,000, Wewak 9,000, with another division arriving. Consider it prudent to forstall enemy by increasing garrison Wau . . . intend to put in reinforcements . . .' Blamey promised him three fresh brigades.

To improve the supply position for the projected assault on Lae, construction began on a jeep road from Bulldog to Wau which was the junction of communicating roads and tracks leading north-east to Salamaua and north to the Markham Valley. Some sixty miles of road had to be formed from Bulldog over ranges as high as 9,800 feet, across country that sometimes shook in quake, dislodging great wads of earth which could carry with them trees that continued to thrive in their new position; cliffs rose up to 1,000 feet and on most days rain fell in torrents. The 14th, 9th and 2/16th field companies employed hundreds of willing natives on this remarkable project. One of the problems was the disappearance of tools, as one of the surveyors reported: 'Loss of tools and pilfering were

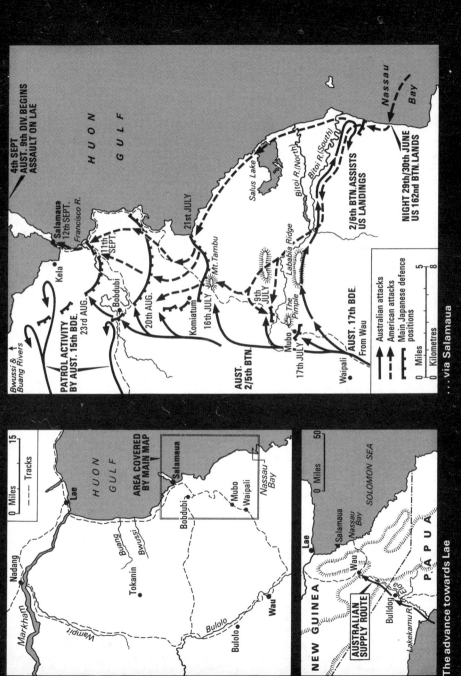

4th SEPT. AUST. 9th DIV. BEGINS ASSAULT ON LAE

H U O N G U L F

Salamaua 12th SEPT.

Francisco R.

Kela •

Bwussi & Buang Rivers

PATROL ACTIVITY BY AUST. 15th BDE. 23rd AUG.

11th SEPT.

Bobdubi

20th AUG.

21st JULY

Salus Lake

Komiatum

16th JULY

Mt. Tambu

9th JULY

Lababia Ridge

Bitoi R. (North)

Bitoi R. (South)

2/6th BTN. ASSISTS US LANDINGS

Nassau

Nassau Bay

AUST. 2/5th BTN.

Mubo

17th JULY

The Pimple

Waipali •

AUST. 17th BDE. From Wau

NIGHT 29th/30th JUNE US 162nd BTN. LANDS

→ Australian attacks
⇢ American attacks
▙ Main Japanese defence positions

0 Miles 5
0 Kilometres 8

H U O N G U L F

0 Miles 15
--- Tracks

Lae •

Nadang •

Markham

Wampit

Tokanin •

Buang
Bwussi

AREA COVERED BY MAIN MAP

Salamaua

Bobdubi •
Mubo •
Waipali •
Nassau Bay

Bulolo

Bulolo •

Wau •

NEW GUINEA

0 Miles 50

SOLOMON SEA

Lae •

Salamaua
Nassau Bay

Wau

AUSTRALIAN SUPPLY ROUTE

Bulldog •

Lakekamu R.

P A P U A

. . . via Salamaua

The advance towards Lae

common. Stores, coming into Bulldog, had been opened and pilfered before their arrival. The Kukukuku tribes along the Eroa are born thieves, and they got away with much equipment. Axes and knives particularly attracted them (and, later, explosives) though they were partial to anything metallic or edible. One party came proudly back to the track on one occasion decorated with detonators through their noses.'

Whatever possibility there was of the Japanese moving in strength on Wau was shattered at the beginning of March by an air attack on a convoy coming from Rabaul. This attack, which became known as the Battle of the Bismarck Sea, sealed the enemy's fate in Papua-New Guinea and demonstrated the superior position of Allied air power. Allied Intelligence had predicted the size, strength and direction of the convoy of eight reinforcement-carrying transports and eight escorting destroyers. RAAF and USAAF aircraft were given sufficient time to gather their forces for the kill, in an area suitable for short-range as well as medium and long-range fighters and bombers. In addition to recce and escort aircraft, the attackers flew thirty-seven heavy bombers, forty-nine medium and light bombers, and ninety-five fighters: Flying Fortresses, Liberators, Mitchells, Bostons (Havocs), Beaufighters and Lightnings. On the morning of the 3rd, Lae airfield was heavily attacked by low-flying Bostons to keep the Zeros there busy or out of action, while the convoy was attacked by Fortresses which sank a transport that stayed afloat long enough to transfer its troops to a destroyer which rushed them to Lae. The next day, B-25 Mitchell bombers, employing the newly-introduced method of skipping bombs off the sea into the sides of ships, caused the most damage. Mitchells followed Beaufighters strafing decks and bridges with their four nose cannon and six wing machine-guns. Every transport was sunk and so were four of the destroyers. The crews of the destroyers and about 2,700 from the transports were saved, but 3,000 were killed or drowned. Allied aircraft losses were light: a Fortress, three Lightnings and a crash-landed Beaufighter. The enemy air force lost several Zeros in the air and more on the ground at Lae. During the month the enemy attempted several retaliatory attacks on Allied bases, from Oro Bay to Port Moresby, and their loss of fighters and bombers was more serious than the damage they caused to Allied shipping and airfields.

There was still a faint possibility of a threat to Australia from Japanese troops based at Timor, a threat which lessened as Darwin's air strips filled with fighters and bombers. Also, Australian and Dutch troops cut off on the island kept the enemy busy and were able to observe his movements and report back through a radio dropped by their regular food suppliers – RAAF Hudsons. The troops were a very ragged lot, usually hungry, but well armed and keen to fight a guerilla war against Timor's occupiers. David Ross, Australian Consul at Dili, had been captured and was sent in March 1942 by the Japanese commander to contact the guerillas and demand their surrender. Ross used this opportunity to pass on his knowledge of Japanese positions and sign official notes for buying food from the locals. He was sent out again in June by the Japanese with a note to the Australian commander, guaranteeing proper treatment if they would surrender; if not, they should 'come to Dili and fight it out man to the last man' or the Japanese commander would take his men into the hills and fight it out there. This time Ross delivered the message and stayed with the guerillas. At the same time, the Portuguese authorities were having trouble with rebel natives, a local affair in which the Australians were not involved and were merely onlookers as loyal natives aided Portu-

guese troops to maintain order. A commando diarist wrote; 'One of our patrols near Mape, out hunting the Jap, encountered a Portuguese patrol out hunting some natives; they exchanged compliments and went on their way. Coy HQ witnessed the spectacle of about 3,000 natives, all in war dress and armed to the teeth, also complete with drums and Portuguese flags, returning from the hunt with many of them nonchalantly swinging heads of the unfortunate in battle.' Instead of surrendering or evacuating after the enemy garrison was reinforced, the guerillas received more commandos into their midst (carried across the Timor Sea by the destroyer HMAS *Voyager* which ran aground and was later scuttled) to keep the 12,000 Japanese troops busy on Timor – when they could have been sent to New Guinea. The odds, however, were against the Allies staying on Timor for the duration and the last evacuation transport – a submarine –

Friendly natives and Australians harass the Japanese garrison on Timor

moved away from the island in February, 1943.

While the New Guinea fighting reached a stalemate after the Japanese retreat from Wau, GHQ was implementing plans to satisfy its grand strategy. Forces under MacArthur, as decided by Washington, were to take Salamaua, Lae and the whole Huon Peninsula, establish air bases on Kiriwina and Woodlark Island, and occupy western New Britain to contain Rabaul. General Blamey was proving his worth as a sagacious tactician and continued to direct the war in New Guinea. He chose Nassau Bay, ten miles south of Salamaua, as his linking position for a concerted New Guinea front and issued orders for the next move on land – the development of airfields in the Markham Valley and the assault on Lae.

Advances

The first Pacific D-Days got away to hopeful starts, while in the other war zone – of which the jungle-clad troops heard through radio broadcasts, including Tokyo Rose's, and army bulletins – the Allies invaded Italy and Sicily, and the Russians began a winter offensive that was to bring increasing successes through spring and summer. This would have been the time for the Japanese leaders to logically and humanely accept defeat and unconditional surrender. If the Japanese god-emperor's position had then been guaranteed by the Allies,

perhaps they would have surrendered, although the Tojo clique maintained a powerful position and were prepared to fight until their country, like Germany, was reduced to a shambles.

In September 1942, Australian Intelligence staff offered a very accurate prediction to Allied Land Headquarters (LHQ) regarding Japan's war policy: because of her limited air strength, Japan could conduct only one offensive – in the SWPA – and would not attack Russia or India; a strategic barrier north of Australia would be complete with the occupa-

tion of New Guinea and, possibly, Darwin and the north-east coast of Australia; her occupied countries would be strengthened so that should Germany be defeated, the exhausted and war-weary Allies would agree to a negotiated peace.

Japan's build-up in the Indies was estimated to have reached about 118,000 and in the New Guinea-Solomons area about 105,000, during the early months of 1943. There were three divisions in the Solomons and three in New Guinea – Seventeenth Army and Eighteenth Army, each the

Opposite: In order to build vital airstrips Kiriwina Island is captured
Above: The wounded trickle back during the advance on Salamaua

equivalent of a British or American corps. They had the support of about 400 serviceable combat aircraft, and a navy slightly weaker than Halsey's fleet. An accurate knowledge of the Japanese army composition and deployment was given to Australian Intelligence staff as a result of the disaster which befell Japan in the Bismarck Sea. Some survivors from the convoy landed on Goodenough Island where they were killed or captured by a garrison militia battallion. A patrol ambushed a group of eight who had landed from two flat-bottomed boats, saw by the badges on the dead that they were staff officers and deduced correctly that some official-looking boxes in the boats would contain valuable information. Inside were documents which included a complete army list of officers and their units, and a summation of the whole army. From earlier fighting, Intelligence had badges from fallen troops (the Allies discarded their unit badges before action) and the Japanese soldier was an inveterate diarist, but information gleaned from this evidence was incomplete; from the Goodenough boxes, Intelligence was able to fill in the missing units.

Halsey had seven infantry divisions at his disposal for the Solomons and and other islands, and MacArthur had two American and twelve Australian divisions. The New Guinea offensives would be fought primarily by Australians whose total armed forces were to grow to almost 500,000, draining too many essential technicians from a population of only 7,000,000. American troops were to be trained for Task Force operations. In General Kenny's Fifth Air Force were 1,400 aircraft, approximately half flown by USAAF, half by RAAF. Two armoured divisions and nine infantry divisions were stationed in Australia and, in March 1943, there were three infantry divisions employed in the holding war in New Guinea. Constitutional use of the militia was altered with the passing, in February, of the Defence (Citizen Military) Act 1943, extending the area of operations for conscripts as far north as the equator. Militia units were strengthened with AIF officers and NCO's, a great many militiamen transferred to the AIF (and gained an 'X' to their number: AIF numbers were prefixed by a letter denoting their enlistment State – e.g. NX 7978 would be the number of

an AIF man enlisted in New South Wales) and some experienced militi-men, who might have transferred, retained their status because of pride in their battalion. Eight militia and fifteen AIF battalions had gained battle experience in New Guinea and there were enough survivors to ensure strength of morale and spirit when they were reinforced, some of them almost totally. The boss of New Guinea Force in April was Lieutenant-General MacKay, and the man sent to direct operations from Wau was Major-General Stanley Savige, who had commanded the 17th Brigade in the Middle East and who had been one of the planners responsible for strengthening the now obsolete, unused 'Brisbane Line'. Savige had an instinct for good officers and men, and stubbornly refused to accept officers recommended by politicians or other influential citizens. The men held for him an affectionate, loyal respect.

With the arrival of the 3rd Division at Wau, Kanga Force was dissolved; the opportunities for guerilla tactics were now more limited as both sides built up their strength to divisions. There would be the old narrow-track fronts and the heartbreaking large assaults against wide, fortified barriers. By the end of April, the 3rd Division, 17th Brigade and three Independent companies were on a long hooked perimeter, extending from the Markham down through the ranges about twenty miles inland, and swinging in from Wau to Mubo, ending at the Francisco river where 2/3rd Independent patrolled the jungle.

At Mubo the enemy had been re-inforced, the Japanese commander believing that the halted Australians had reached the end of their tether, and severe fighting developed across the enemy's line of supply. The fight for 'the Pimple', a high peak, was particularly bloody when the 2/7th Battalion climbed up to take it. The commandos maintained a cheeky pressure against the enemy from a

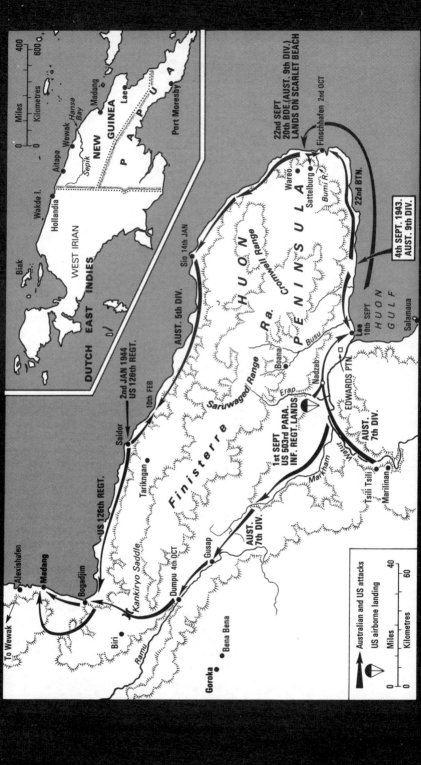

Opposite: Into Salamaua; American and Australian troops cross the Fransisco *Above:* A captured Japanese gun being used against Salamaua. *Below:* The continuous assault on Japanese-held Salamaua

ridge only a couple of miles from Salamaua until he brought up a strong battalion, supported by heavy artillery and mortar fire, against the company. For a small loss to themselves the commandos inflicted a great number of casualties among the Japs who desperately called up fighters from Lae which, however, strafed and bombed empty positions and, watched by the Australians, attacked an extensive area occupied by Japanese. This kind of work by the Independents was raising their image in the ranks of AIF veterans, who were inclined to scoff at the 'do or die' attitudes expressed by beretted commandos in training.

The infantryman was going into action better equipped than he was in 1942. One item had not changed: the wide-brimmed felt hat, creased, battered, or twisted into a infinite variety of shapes, and worn in pref-

erence to the steel helmet. His uniform was green, from gaiters to shirt and webbing equipment; he packed a spare pair of brown boots, sox, singlet, shirt, trousers and green mosquito net in a pack; he carried a water bottle on one side of his belt and on the other a haversack containing rations: emergency, field operation and one day's ordinary – all of them simply bully beef and biscuits – mess gear, towel, mosquito-repellent, toilet gear and atebrin tablets. Around the pack, which was left at company or battalion headquarters when there was action, was wrapped his blankets and groundsheet. He carried in pockets in front of his webbing fifty rounds for his rifle, or one hundred for his Thompson or Owen, or one hundred for his Bren. One or two grenades with four-second fuses were hooked by their lever to his webbing belt. He was also required to carry his 'tin hat' but it was usually too much of a nuisance to wear in jungle conditions and was left behind with his pack.

Senior officers explain the position to Sir Leslie Moreshead

Patrolling, with its high incidence of casualties among scouts, was the main activity before a strong point was to be invested with air strikes, gun and mortar barrages, and attack by footsloggers. In the Pimple area the jungle was so thick that a patrol spent a whole day undetected thirty yards from the enemy, listening to them talking, coughing, chopping and rattling mess tins. In the comparatively soldier-empty spaces within the long perimeter, there were Angau men watching the native situation and collating information of enemy movement. John Sherlock, Angau representative based at the isolated village of Mapos, was in a position to learn from his guides and their native contacts where exactly the enemy was patrolling in the Buang and Bwussi rivers area. The extensive network of Allied agents throughout the area was a valuable addition to aerial photography which was now peering so closely into the enemy's camp. Aircraft and ground observers also detected the movement of barges and destroyers bringing up Japanese reinforcements during April and May – about 1,800 of them, 400 arriving in submarines. Coast watchers in the mountains above the Markham reported enemy patrols in the Wain mountains, a branch of the Finisterre Range which ran out into spurs through the Huon Peninsula; patrols which were also contributing to the survey of a land route from Lae to Madang. The Allies' main interest in the Markham Valley was its suitability for airfields, particularly the Nadzab area.

By 'feinting' towards Salamaua and grabbing Nassau Bay, Blamey hoped to lead the enemy to drain some of his strength from Lae. Whichever thrust was made – real or pretended – the result was going to be a bloody battle. To General Adachi, Salamaua was a very important strategic position, to be held at all costs and defended to the last man; should Salamaua fall he believed that Lae would be lost, and so, when Blamey's feint began, as well as drawing troops from Rabaul and Wewak, Adachi did bring some up from Lae. He had supply problems in bringing food and materials across the sea to his bases, whereas Blamey had the benefit of a number of Dakota squadrons, 'biscuit bombers', which supplemented the supply line through Bulldog. The Dakotas and their cargo loads were to leave a lasting impression on the natives who, on first seeing the aircraft, asked whether they were male or female. Once Nassau Bay was occupied, the Allied supply position would improve.

In June, the 2/7th sent patrols into the Bay area to estimate enemy strength and positions, and the 2/6th clashed with the enemy in several severe fights which always resulted in the enemy losing many more than the Australians. In these jungle clashes, where the enemy was screened, the grenade was proving to be the most effective weapon, both the four-second grenade hurled by hand and the seven-second fired from a discharger. In close encounters out in the open it was grenades, rifles and automatics that checked and drove back the enemy. During the main engagement near Mubo, at Lababia Ridge, 150 men of the 2/6th were attacked by 1,500 of the Japanese 66th Infantry Regiment: in a couple of days the Japanese suffered nearly 200 casualties while the Australians lost eleven killed and twelve wounded. Such expertise gave the Australians great confidence, even in situations where they were surrounded.

The fight at Lababia Ridge proved to the enemy that he had little hope of ever getting to Wau. General Nakano, 51st Division commander, and Colonel Araki, who directed the 66th, had been confident that the Australians would be driven out of the area. On the 19th, they believed that 'tomorrow at dawn we will start mopping up with entire strength and will destroy the enemy (at Lababia).

We will then continue on to Guadagasal. The enemy appears not to be aware of our plans, he is sunbathing at Guadagasal.' They were shocked and dismayed when they found the Australian position impenetrable, not because of strong log-emplacements which was the Japanese formula for defence, but because of a clever use of non-concealment. Approaching uphill, the Japanese could not see the defence positions hidden behind trees; once they were on top of the rise they could clearly see ahead beneath the trees, for the leaves, branches and shrubs had been cleared from the ground up to a height of about four feet. This area was now a thin maze of tree trunks through which the Australians had many clear fields of fire. When Japanese who survived the booby-traps attacked. they were shot down and were forced to abandon the attack.

From Lababia the 2/6th infiltrated parties down to assist the landing at Nassau Bay by the 1/162nd US Battalion who were brought in by boats of the 2nd Engineer Special Brigade ('Cape Cod Commandos') on the night of 29-30th June. It was a landing in rough surf, confusion and congestion, but generally safe, and the infantrymen went on their first skirmishes at daylight. When night fell after their first day in light contact with the enemy, anyone moving in the dark was thought to be an infiltrating enemy, and the night was brightened by tracer, grenade and mortar explosions. A 2/6th officer said 'my blokes went to ground and stayed there.' A Papuan rifle company was also aiding the landing by attacking Japanese positions on the left flank. The beach-head was established without much interference from the enemy and within a month there were over 1,400 Americans at Nassau Bay. The enemy escaped to Salamaua, except for the few who stayed to fight and die. One Japanese sergeant went down from the jungle where he had been cut off and, instead of *hara-kiri* or *banzai*, preferred to

stay alive when he found tins of beef, milk, peaches and bread in an unguarded US store.

While Nassau Bay was being successfully inhabited, Mubo was attacked and won, after a week of bitter fighting by the 17th Brigade. The 58th/59th militiamen fought for Bobdubi in the commandos' area near Salamaua, a fight that developed into a long series of patrols and skirmishes, over ridge and valley country, and for a while distracted the enemy from Mubo. The battle for that unpleasant, unhealthy piece of mountain country lasted until 13th July, and when it was lost to the 17th Brigade, who had the valuable assistance of a force from the US regiment on one flank, General Nakano realised that, 'the Lae-Salamaua area is at the very limit of this decisive struggle, and upon the decision in this fight, the whole fate of our Empire depends. The strongholds of Lae and Salamaua must be defended to the death.'

The feint against Salamaua continued to be realistically strong. In moving closer along the coast so that American guns could be emplaced on the high ground of Mount Tambu, overlooking Salamaua, there was some bitter fighting for 162nd Regiment combat teams. One, under a Major Roosevelt, was disorganised mainly because the CO resented having to cooperate with his Australian superiors. Roosevelt was so uncooperative that Captain Sturrock, the liaison officer, was quite astounded: 'Am most unpopular over trying to get information re future operations and sitreps [situation reports]. The only way I can get information is to remain within battalion headquarters area and listen in to phone conversations . . . the organisation at battalion headquarters stinks . . . if the show continues as it is now I can't see them getting very far.'

The 2/5th Battalion, down from the hard fighting at Mobu, was sent in on a flank towards Mount Tambu and into another period of battle. In David

Dexter's official history, *The New Guinea Offensives*, he describes a night and a day that were typical of so many during the struggle for the ridges: 'In the evening a severe earth tremor startled the troops . . . rained heavily . . . did not deter the Japanese from moving in darkness from Mount Tambu to the flanks of the two companies of the 2/5th. Despite the torrential downpour . . . the rear platoon heard noises . . . the Japanese charge out of the darkness. A defending Bren gunner, with a lucky burst into the darkness, knocked out the raiders' machine-gun which had been firing along the track into the centre of the Australian position. All enemy attempts to recapture their machine-gun resulted in their dead being piled up along the track . . . withdrew before first light leaving 21 dead . . . Sporadic attacks continued during the day . . . Japanese increased the din of battle with screaming and yelling, for example: "Come out and fight, you Aussie conscripts," and "Come out

A convoy for the sea-borne assault on Lae

and die for Tojo" . . . determination and experience of a seasoned unit (actually AIF, not conscripted militia) prevailed. Walters (2/5th) reported: "By 2.30 that day we knew we had him. Our men stood up in their trenches, and sometimes out of them, yelling back the Japs' own war cry and often quaint ones of their own. One of them knew a smattering of Japanese and had a great time, shouting out such things as 'Ten minutes smoke, lads.' It developed into an absolute slaughter and we literally belted him into the ground" . . . rounds fired by the mountain guns and the supporting mortar fire had been invaluable in breaking up the attacks.'

Patrolling against a stationary enemy in the Tambu area produced intense action at Ambush Knoll, one of the many points which acquired a name as a result of groups of men digging holes and trying to kill one

121

another. When the troops became exhausted, they were sent up to the Wau-Bulolo valley to rest for a couple of weeks then brought back to the jungle. The Americans and Australians continued their fight for these dominating ridges and for the space in front of Salamaua during the next few weeks, by which time both sides knew every possible track through the jungle. In the guerilla trials, the Allies won the psychological objective desired by NGHQ – to lead the enemy into believing that Lae was to be the secondary target.

Beyond the headwaters of the Markham, which flowed east to Lae, and the headwaters of the Ramu, which flowed north-west to the Bismark Sea, there was a plateau that

Right: Adachi's escape route to the Finisterres cut by the airdrop on Nadzab. *Below:* The Japanese under air attack at Lae. *Bottom opposite:* Heavy equipment can now be brought up to Nadzab for the drive on Lae

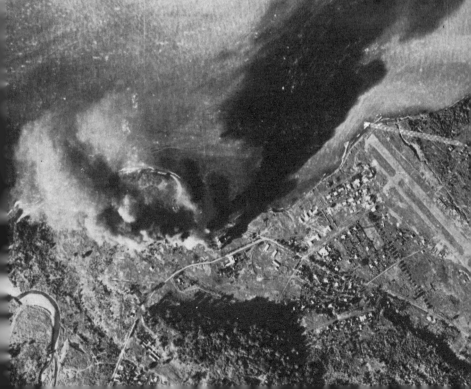

could be of use to either side. This time the Allies were first in with a strong enough force to establish bases at Dumpu, Goroka, Tsili Tsili (pronounced 'silly silly') and the old airstrip at Bena Bena – a vast mosquito-free area which had rarely been visited by white men. At Goroka, amazingly skilful American engineers employed 1,000 natives and built a 600-foot long airstrip, with dispersal bays, in seven days. All the time these developments were taking place, the enemy was prodding into the Ramu and there were skirmishes and hair-raising clashes in the weird countryside. Gradually the bow-and-arrow warriors of the plateau could see who was stronger and became more friendly towards the white men, offering labour and information.

In June and July two islands – Kiriwina and Woodlark – were safely reinforced by US Cavalrymen who helped prepare airstrips; USAAF Lightening fighters flew in to Woodlark and 79 Squadron RAAF Spitfires flew in to Kiriwina. Thus there were two fighter bases protecting the south-east approaches to Papua and near enough to New Britain to provide escorts for bombers attacking Gasmata and Rabaul.

To capture Lae, Blamey planned to send the AIF 7th Division down the Markham valley and bring the AIF 9th Division in to make a landing from the sea. When the 9th had remained in the Middle East its commander, Major-General Morshead, had inherited Blamey's charter which gave the Australians the right to decide where they should fight. The British command had wanted to split the division to use its brigades in different operations but Morshead had insisted on them remaining as a unified division. The 9th had stopped and held the Germans at Tobruk in 1941 and, in October 1942, fought at El Alamein where, Montgomery had said, the battle would have been lost without the division. Morshead, with more experience in desert warfare than

Montgomery, Alexander or Lumsden (an Eighth Army corps commander), should have been promoted to corps leadership but Montgomery told him that, not being a regular soldier, he did not possess 'the requisite training and experience', an attitude Blamey described as 'unconscious arrogance'. It was not, however, because of this attitude to Morshead, but because the division was needed in Australia that it was recalled after El Alamein, again despite Churchill's eagerness for the division to remain in the Eighth Army.

Regarding the coming battle that the two AIF divisions were to fight, Blamey wrote: 'The fulfilment of the offensive plan contemplated the establishment of air superiority, the softening of enemy resistance by continued air attacks on the successive objectives of the land forces, and, by attacking enemy shipping, forward bases and airfields, the interruption to reinforcement and supply of enemy forces.' The Fifth Air Force – the USAAF and RAAF force – had increased its strength, particularly in medium bombers, and the enemy brought its 7th Air Division down to New Guinea from the NEI. By the end of July, Japan had two air divisions supporting her army in New Guinea and nearby islands, with main air bases at Rabaul, the Admiralties, Wewak, Hansa Bay, But, Boikin, Aitape and Hollandia. These were all within medium-bomber range of the Allies who planned to build airstrips close enough to Lae so that fighters could cover airborne and seaborne movement of troops.

Much of the patrolling during May was for the purpose of investigating areas suitable for airstrips. Marilinan and Tsili Tsili, on the Watut, were ideal for there was a reasonable jeep track on the edge of the valley, a track which crossed a bridge built by Warrant Officer Lumb. Lumb had rounded up cattle and overlanded them along the track and over the bridge when the Japanese had first

come ashore at Lae. When the airstrips were ready in June, fighters flew in to cover the Dakotas bringing in troops, equipment and supplies. The next move was down the Markham to Nadzab where more strips could be built; the 7th Division could then be given greater support and supply facilities, while they fulfilled their dual purpose of cutting off the possibility of enemy reinforcement from over the range and attacking Lae.

Nadzab would be taken by US paratroops dropped over the area and AIF troops air transported to Tsili Tsili and marched down the valley, fording the Markham on the way. The urging from GHQ was now more subtle, the nervousness dissipated; in fact, there was an air of confidence as thousands of tons of stores and equipment were sent up for the first big push – and the attack on Lae was carried out on a comparatively grand scale.

Before that attack was mounted, however, Americans and Australians

Australian troops march into Lae, an important Japanese stronghold

had managed to take their ridges near Salamaua and chase the enemy back towards the base. General Savige encouraged the pursuit but he did not want the enemy running from Salamaua to Lae. 15th Brigade chased the enemy by day and, in Japanese fashion, by night, lowering his morale, spoiling his sleep and keeping him jittery. The Americans made their moves along a ridge which followed the coastline for a couple of miles and, for both allies, the move towards Salamaua from 26th August to 10th September was through rough, hilly, jungle country. Brigadier H H Hammer commanded 15th Brigade and planned the assault on Salamaua. He was especially pleased with the militiamen, '. . . magnificent, many sick refused to be evacuated – they knew the unit strengths were low and they preferred to remain and continue the fight . . .' who were perhaps inspired by their companions, the 2/7th Battalion. An attempt was made to get the enemy to surrender: an American, Lieutenant Bowers, used a loudspeaker in a forward trench, broadcasting in Japanese, but although the enemy listened quietly to the speech none came forward.

On 10th September, six days after D-Day at Lae, resistance collapsed south of the Francisco river and that night there was an increase in the barge traffic between Lae and Salamaua. Also, enemy wireless conversations had stopped that night, suggesting that the Salamaua commander had also taken a boat ride up to Lae. The following day it was decided that the Americans should have the honour of taking Salamaua, but they were at first delayed, and then held up by the flooded Francisco river. Anyway, a company of the 42nd militia swam the river, occupied the airstrip at 9.30am, without opposition, and then, suffering the loss of eight men killed, took Salamaua. The 1/162nd moved in the following day. That battalion, which had fought so hard with their regiment against a determined enemy and under the most frightful conditions, was awarded a presidential citation. The seven-month campaign that ended with the fall of swampy, filthy, pestilential Salamaua cost heavy casualties, most of them through illness. From the end of June to 12th September, the Americans lost eighty-one killed and 396 wounded 15th Brigade lost 112 killed, 346 wounded and twelve missing; the enemy lost 762 killed by the brigade during that period and, in the period from April to August, suffered about 8,000 casualties. 5,000 Japanese escaped by barge to Lae, 600 by submarine to Rabaul and about 200 overland to Lae.

From Lae, at the mouth of the Markham, the Huon Gulf coastline runs east and south. Lae and its airstrip are on the northern bank of the river, opposite extensive swamps. On 1st September, the first of many impressive SWPA convoys was on its way to Lae – destroyers, LST's, LCI's and LCT's carrying men of the 20th Brigade, advance force of the 9th Division. They arrived on the 4th, landing at two beaches some fifteen miles from Lae. The landing was unopposed, except by Zeros and bombers which caused a few casualties, and while the infantry moved out to secure the beach-head, an American shore battalion and American and Australian engineers landed to establish a base and commence building roads: the equipment that arrived with the boats included everything from bullets to bulldozers. The unloading speed was amazing, the highly trained Americans getting 400 men, thirty-five vehicles and eighty tons of bulk stores off an LST within about two hours. US destroyer *Reid*, which had long been operating in the Huon Gulf as a floating radar station, called up Lightnings to intercept a large raid in which the Japanese lost about twenty-three aircraft. The enemy were more successful against six LST's still at sea, carrying the second landing group of 2/4th Independent Company and 2/2nd Machine Gun Battalion: they seriously damaged two of the craft, killing fifty-one and wounding sixty-seven sailors and troops. By the 6th, General Wooten had three brigades of his 9th Division safely ashore and advancing towards Lae.

The use of paratroops in the Markham Valley brought a certain amount of despair to the Japanese commanders who had hoped to be able to use the valley as a highway up to the Finisterres. The US 503rd Parachute Infantry Regiment were dropped near the junction of the Erap and Markham on 1st September. It had been decided that a few AIF short 25-pounders would be useful so 2/4th Field Regiment gunners were asked to volunteer to jump with them; they were given a quick course in the procedures of leaping out of aeroplanes; some had never made a jump until in the actual operation they floated down with the paratroops. One was injured as were thirty-three Americans; three other paratroops were killed when their chutes failed to open. The Australians were amused to be dubbed by their American friends, 'the two-bar-four Airborne Cannon Company'.

Another mishap occurred when the 7th Division AIF were emplaning at Jackson Field, Port Moresby, to fly into Nadzab on the 7th. Five trucks carrying troops were hit by a bomb laden Liberator crashing on take-off; fifty-nine were killed or died of injuries and ninety-two were injured, and the eleven crew members of the bomber were killed. Three days of bad weather delayed the air-lift to the wide kunai grass plain of the Markham Valley and it wasn't until the 5th that the division could march along the river valley to confront the Lae garrison.

The 9th Division had been held up by the swollen Busu river where bridging had to be brought up and constructed. The delay gave the main battle honours to the 7th Division who were able to move down from Nadzab without much opposition. While Salamaua was falling, the 7th Division infantry, engineers, artillery, pioneers, American paratroops and Papuans were assembling, slowly because of bad weather, on the broad plain of the Markham. They began to fight their way down-river on the 12th – while the 9th Division were still held up at the Busu and were drawing enemy action to themselves – and while a force moved over from Watut and attacked Markham Point from the south. Again it was sections and platoons, and a few individuals in each, that wrested enemy strong-points after close fighting. III Battalion of the American paratroops went to the headwaters of the Bumbu to block Japanese withdrawals, for it was evident that the enemy was planning to flee rather than fight in Lae to the last man. Already there were reports of Japanese arriving at Boana, a village in the hills below the Wain range, a branch of the Finisterre-Saruwaged-Cromwell ranges. To get across those ranges to the Madang coast from Boana was a feat difficult enough for an experienced, unloaded native; it would prove fatal to many of the exhausted and ill-fed Japanese. To stop the withdrawal movement, General Wooten deployed some of his companies through areas where he expected resistance and found them abandoned.

As both divisions drew together for the kill, the enemy fought delaying actions while he withdrew along obscure tracks surveyed weeks before. There were stronger positions for the 7th to overcome along the Markham, notably at a place known as Edwards' Plantation. On 16th September, the town, 'indescribably filthy and thoroughly wrecked', was taken after the 7th suffered unnecessary casualties resulting from a strafing attack by USAAF aircraft, and from a shelling by the 9th artillery. The airfield was overgrown and a shambles, and had that typical nauseating stench of an area occupied by a besieged Japanese army.

The 9th Division had not been worked very hard in its first encounter with Japanese and were inclined to scoff at their resistance: 'The enemy has done nothing to entitle him to our respect during the operation and his performance indicates that he is not as good as the Italian as a fighting man,' wrote one battalion historian. They were to learn differently in the near future. In one of their encounters they had willingly gone in with the bayonet, and generally there was no holding back. The 9th lost seventy-seven killed, seventy-three missing and nearly 400 wounded; the 7th lost thirty-eight killed, 104 wounded; and the Japanese lost about 2,000. If it hadn't been for the unexpected flooding of the Busu, another 6,000 would have died instead of escaping across the mountains. They were hurried in their retreat by the 7th Division who took Dumpu, in

the Ramu Valley and by the 9th Division, who mopped up around Lae to secure the base. The fighting spirit had gone out of the enemy and, although there were few surrenders, parties of them scattered when fired upon as they made their strenuous withdrawal.

However, there were suprises: the 2/6th Independent Company destroyed a force of about sixty enemy who were thought to be withdrawing from Lae; instead they were the vanguard of the Japanese 78th Regiment and a 75mm artillery battalion which had originally been despatched to take Bena Bena. The rest of their division, the 20th, were sent on to Finschhafen while the vanguard was driven back into the mountains by the 2/14th Battalion and 2/6th commandos. While the Allies were out-manoeuvring the enemy with the use of air transport, the enemy had gone some way towards modern transportation by building a road from Bogadjim over the Finisterres; before it could be finished, they were battling in the mountains to stop the Allies rolling down to the coast.

Madang, then Wewak were the next largest enemy bases along the coast of New Guinea and the geography of the Huon Peninsula dictated the moves. Two militia divisions, 5th and 11th, would be brought in to continue the fight with the two AIF divisions moving in two main directions against the Japanese: around the coast via Finschhafen, and across from Ramu to Bogadjim.

Sattelberg

The strategic agenda for operations in the SWPA was running according to plan, and it looked as though all objectives would be taken by the end of the year. The north-west coast of New Guinea was under attack by September and, after pushing the last Japanese out of New Georgia in August, US forces landed on the last major target in the Solomons – Bougainville – on 1st November. Rabaul, a former primary target for invasion and recapture, was relegated to the obscurity of a by-passed area that could be contained and mopped up when time and surplus bombs could be 'wasted'. Once MacArthur could free himself from the New Guinea commitment, he would gather his American divisions and advance totowards the Philippines, while in the Central Pacific, the Joint Chiefs of Staff agreed, assaults against the Gilbert Islands and Nauru should commence before the end of the year. On the 20th November, US Marines landed at Makin and Tarawa in the Gilberts.

The Japanese could not linger for long in the inhospitable mountains

beyond the Markham and Ramu headwaters, nor could the Allies leave such a large pocket as Finschhafen in enemy hands. The successful sea-borne assault on the beaches near Lae encouraged Blamey and MacArthur to again employ Rear-Admiral Daniel E Barbey's little Seventh Amphibious Fleet to carry the 9th Division on its next operation. Finschhafen was a stronger base after Lae fell – some troops from Lae walked there or were carried by barge, and others were sent up from Bogadjim, Sio and Saidor. Scarlet

Opposite: The devastation at Sattelberg after the Allied onslaught. *Above:* The wounded are brought out of Sattelberg

Beach, where the 20th Brigade were to land, was strongly fortified, but fortunately the landing craft deposited the Australians on wrong beaches, before dawn on 22nd September, and they were able to move in behind Scarlet Beach and secure the beach-head. Another piece of luck was that the landing craft guns were used, against orders, as the craft

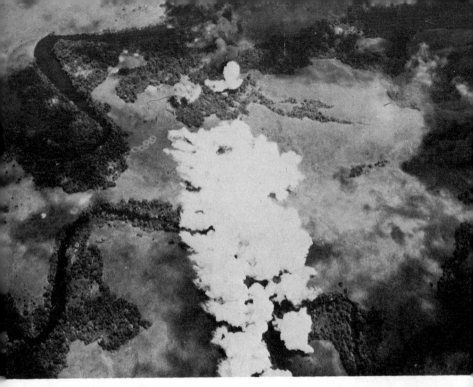

moved in and their fire proved very useful. Patrolling Lightnings were on the spot when Barbey's boats were attacked by some forty enemy aircraft; thirty-eight were claimed by gunners and Lightning pilots.

The US Admiral believed that Finschhafen was lightly held and, for a while, refused to provide transport for a second Australian brigade, the 24th; he was eventually convinced that not only was the fresh Japanese 20th Division, less the 78th Regiment, at Finschhafen, there was also a regiment of infantry, a marine formation and a Naval Base Unit, altogether about 5,000 troops. At the same time as the landings were to be made the 22nd militia began a move roun the coast. At Finschhafen the coastal ledge was very narrow and the harbour and airstrip were close to towering foothills of the Cromwell Mountains. The Japanese had the advantages of fortifications and height. From where the Australians landed a road wound up into the mountains for about

eight miles to the village of Sattelberg; and another, partly-formed, road led along the coast to Finschhafen. The first main obstacle on the approach along the coast was the Bumi river where the enemy was entrenched on the southern bank. Going upstream through the bush to fight for a bridgehead was an incredible feat, as the official historian describes:

'The men of the 2/15th's two assaulting companies literally fell for the first 150 yards from their start-line. Tumbling over vines, crashing through bamboo and heavy timber, the men stumbled to the bottom of the valley. About 450 yards from the start they came to a precipitous slope. Pulling themselves up hand over hand for about 200 feet, their training and stamina came to their aid so that near the summit the formation was maintained and the companies advanced upwards on a front of about 150 yards.'

On top of the hill was a company of what were regarded as Japan's *corps d'élite* – the marines. Faced with the Australians' unfaltering advance upwards, the marines began to shower them with grenades which fortunately were largely ineffective. Had they been good grenades, the attacking companies would have suffered heavy losses. Corporal Norris, a Queensland cattle station overseer, leading the first section of Snell's company, was blown down the hill by a grenade landing a foot away. He picked himself up and climbed back to lead the assault; most of the fire passed over the Queenslanders as their relentless advance continued, not yet using grenades which would have rolled back on them. Cold steel flashed as the Australians came to the summit and charged with their bayonets. Most of the Japanese, taller than average,

turned and fled. The river was crossed, the men up to their waists and fired on as they forded to establish a bridgehead.

Finschhafen and its harbour were captured on 2nd October, and contact was made with the coast-trekking 22nd Battalion. This achievement had been hard fought and there was stiffer fighting to come. The main enemy force, 20th Division, was still out in the country where they intended to make their main stand. General Wooten expected strong counter-attacks and hoped to reduce the enemy's numbers by preparing for them. He was helped when Intelligence found, on the body of a Japanese officer, a copy of the order for a counter-attack. That attack was made on Jivevenang, about half-way to Sattelberg, on 16th October; the following day, enemy aircraft raided while an amphibious assault was attempted towards Scarlet Beach. The

first attack was held while the one from the sea was stopped and practically wiped out by fire from infantry anti-aircraft guns and PT boats. Nevertheless, Scarlet Beach came under attack from inland, launched by the Japanese 79th Regiment, and a desperate situation developed for the Australians. The division's 26th Brigade had not arrived and Wooten was running short of reserves; the 24th was cut off for a few days when the enemy infiltrated down to the southern end of Scarlet Beach. The 9th Division men were learning that the Japanese did fight harder than the Italians and were more suicidal than the Germans. By the time the 26th arrived the Australians had lost four killed and 179 wounded, and the Japanese casualties were estimated at over 1,500.

As the Japanese were pushed back into the mountain country, they lost the supply facilities of coastal barges. Their main base was now in an area five miles from the sea and extended

Above: Australian troops on the way up through the Finisterres to take Bogadjim. *Opposite:* Shaggy Ridge

from Sattelberg across the Soni valley to Wareo. Their living conditions deteriorated and the ordinary soldier was, as could be expected, going hungry. 'I eat potatoes and live in a hole' . . . 'What shall I eat to live?' ' . . . the enemy patrol is always wandering around day and night' . . . 'they are probably drinking whisky because they are a rich country and their trucks are able to bring up such desirable things', they wrote in their diaries. The Allies were being supplied by sea from Buna and Lae, the transports protected by PT boats and Lightning fighters against submarine or air attacks, the latter occurring frequently and making LST captains quite twitchy. When a squadron of Matilda tanks of 1st Tank Battalion arrived in three LST's, one of the craft was pulling out from the

Green Sniper's
Pimple

McCaughey's
Knoll·

Faria

Mainstream

River

Above: The Royal Papuan Constabulary in full fighting kit. *Below:* Tanks and infantry take Hollandia from the Japanese. *Bottom:* Rabaul harbour undergoes an Allied air attack

shore while the remaining stores and ammunition were being unloaded – the captain was aiming to be clear of the area before dawn.

As the induced stalemate extended into November, both sides prepared for the battle which was launched by the Australians on 17th November. The heights of Sattelberg were to be cleared before the east ridge running from Wareo to the coast. The 24th Brigade went forward to cut that line while the 26th, supported by tanks, assaulted Sattelberg. Platoons hurled grenades and charged machine-gun posts; mortars reached out for trenches and holes in thick jungle; aggressiveness and luck and extremely accurate fire from the 25-pounders, combined to win the fight for the Australians. The main supply route, from Wareo to Sattelberg had to be cut, an obligation that created a battle situation at a wooded knoll – Pabu – fought over for a week. The Japanese were now fighting as hard as they had ever fought, aggressively and cunningly. General Blamey – and his field commanders – were seeing the result of Admiral Barbey's refusal to bring up the 24th Brigade at the right time so that the enemy could be contained at Finschhafen. Blamey wrote: 'With all due respect to our friends I think this incident shows the weakness of trying to fight battles from a distance with fixed assumptions that the enemy is bent on withdrawal and that he is incapable of increasing the number of his forces. In point of fact, far from withdrawing, his intentions seem to be just the opposite.' Because newspaper correspondents' reports mentioned 'Japanese counter-attacks', and MacArthur's communiques stated 'efforts to break through ... apparently for the purpose of escape,' the war correspondents' reports were censored.

The battle at the knoll and along the Coconut Ridge country towards Sattelberg was fought by the 26th Brigade supported by tanks, guns, mortars and machine-guns. The enemy had quickly dug a series of anti-tank ditches, which were either by-passed or filled in, and had laid anti-tank mines. The tanks slowed the progress of the Australians but they were most useful in knocking out fortified enemy positions. As the Australians swung in towards Sattelberg, the Japanese attacked the 54th Brigade on the coast, moving in from the north. On the morning of 25th November, Sattelberg was found abandoned, after irresistible onslaughts by Australian infantry. During one of these attacks Sergeant T C Derrick, 2/48th Battalion, who had a fighting reputation already established from his days in Tobruk, won his Victoria Cross. To quote the official historian: 'When his platoon was held up Derrick had clambered forward and with grenades had knocked out the post holding up the leading section (Corporal Everett's). He then led forward the second section (Lance-Corporal Connelly's) to attack on the right and when it was halted by fire he scrambled ahead to within six yards of the enemy and threw grenade after grenade at the weapon pits above him . . . led his platoon up the slope with the three sections following one another. It was about 6.45pm. Derrick and his men had a battle on its hands in the Ramu fired with Brens and Owens into the openings of these covered posts at 10 or 12 yards, range and then one man – Derrick in one instance, Private 'Slogger' Sutherland in the other – rushed forward and dropped a grenade in the slit of a post ...'

The loss of Sattelberg and the knoll at Pabu ended Adachi's hopes of recapturing Finschhafen and Lae. He was also surprised to learn that, on 26th December, US Marines landed on New Britain to begin closing the trap on Rabaul and, more seriously to his New Guinea forces, the US 126th Regiment landed at Saidor, nearly one hundred miles ahead of the Australians, effectively cutting off his retreat and coastal supply lines.

Meanwhile, the AIF 7th Division

had a battle on its hands in the Ramu valley and the foothills of the Finisterres where Dumpu and Gusap were tactically important bases. The Australians were winning the skirmishes which developed into static fights on razor-back ridges and pimplehills. A 2/14th Battalion platoon's fight, on 11th October, may not have been typical, but the topography where it took place certainly was. Sergeant Bear and Corporal Silver led their men in an almost perpendicular charge straight up into the enemy position; as they scrambled over the ledge they were seen by a Japanese in a foxhole and both sides missed as they emptied magazines at each other. 'Bear heaved himself straight up over the ledge, lunging with the bayonet in the same movement. He hurled the Japanese like a sheaftosser, then he sprang clear to meet the next foe.' Corporal Whitechurch reported: 'We could see them now and opened fire on their heads as they bobbed up above their foxholes. Their fire began to slacken off. One of our chaps gave a shrill blood-curdling yell that startled even us, and was partly responsible for some of the Japs running headlong down the hill in panic. Unable to stop at the edge of the cliff, they plunged to their doom hundreds of feet below.'

It often occurred in these mountains that the tops and parts of the slopes of ridges were covered in tall kunai grass, a grass which took over and held its ground when jungle was either burnt or cleared away by hand. A most impressive-looking mass of kunai-covered mountain rose from the Faria river and along its top ran Shaggy Ridge. In the fighting beyond the Ramu, this ridge was very important to the Japanese who clung to it desperately, for it led to Kankiryo Saddle which was the gateway to their Bogadjim road. They prepared the ridge with fire lanes burnt through the kunai, the precipitous sides were pocked with dug-in and heavily bunkered positions, there was barbed wire,

and the enemy was prepared to fight to the death. There were also 75mm guns which the Japanese kept in caves, ran out to fire quick salvos then ran back to avoid being spotted by RAAF Wirraway and Boomerang aircraft. The 2/16th Battalion historian described Shaggy Ridge:

'A narrow razor-back with an altitude of 5,000 feet. A thick rain forest covered the crest of the ridge. Heavy mists frequently obscured the position for days at a time. Then observation was limited to less than 100 yards. Such was the vantage point of the eminence that on clear days observation was possible as far as the sea near Madang. The ridge was at no part wider than a few yards narrowing at the foremost section position. The most forward position, a foxhole, was occupied by a lone Bren gunner. For the first time in its history the battalion held ground with a one-man front. Ahead of him was the enemy who had had weeks to prepare his defences.'

Shaggy Ridge, a milder form of Gallipoli's Lone Pine post, was contained while other Japanese positions were attacked and taken during November and December. The enemy was still sweating it out on that high razor-back, half-starved and with little hope, when the Australians had one of the rarest Christmas feasts ever held right in the front line during the second world war: roast turkey, fresh vegetables, plum pudding (with a sauce) and tea and buns. While harrassing fire was maintained on the quaking enemy, the 2/27th's chaplain preached on the seasonal theme, 'Peace on earth and goodwill towards men.'

There was no other alternative, it seemed, than to push ahead on this one-man front against 300-400 enemy stretched back about 400 yards from a high point known as the 'Pimple'. The 2/16th Battalion was supported by enormous fire power when they were given Shaggy Ridge to take – a ghastly Christmas present. Kittyhawk and

Boomerang fighter-bombers worked for twenty minutes with bombs, in ten minutes the guns fired 350 high explosive 25-pound shells Kittyhawks strafed for ninety minutes – before and during the infantry attack – and the guns opened up again, firing 1,400 shells ahead of the infantry as they moved forward, watched by friends and enemies from the tops of other hills and ridges. The Pimple was cleared of jungle by the bombardment but the Japs were still there and Corporal Hall wiped out a pill-box single-handed, enabling the lead platoon to move ahead. General Vasey flew over in a Piper Cub to get a closer view of the little battle on the ridge. The platoon moved forward that Boxing Day until, in the evening, they were held up by fire from a rock bunker at which more than one hundred grenades had been thrown. The following morning, the bunker was destroyed by bombs made of grenades inside chemical-filled field ration tins, and the Japanese officer and one private,

Large quantities of supplies are landed for the Allied assault on Hollandia

who had held up the advance, were killed.

By 3rd January the 18th Brigade, back for another tour of duty in New Guinea, relieved the 21st Brigade which was flown back to Moresby. The 2/9th Battalion took over the front positions, 2/10th on the right, 2/2nd Pioneers on the left and 2/12th in reserve. Shaggy Ridge was cleared on 23rd January.

The enemy had time to dig himself in very strongly, not only on Shaggy Ridge; he was at Geyton's Hill, Canning's Saddle, Cam's Hill and Cam's Saddle. He defended all these positions through various attacks with three battalions of the 78th Regiment; he lost heavily and the Australians lost few by comparison. Adachi had won time for his battalions on the coast but it was futile. When the 7th Division infantry won the pimples, ridges, knolls and saddles, and forced their way past Kankiryo in February, they handed over to the 15th Brigade militiamen to chase the enemy down the Bogadjim road.

Japan was feeling the squeeze from both ends of her collapsing Co-Prosperity Sphere. On 9th January, the Allies overran Maungdaw on the Arakan front in Burma, on the 31st Americans invaded the Marshall Islands, and on 10th February Australian troops linked with Americans at Saidor. The 9th Division had pushed the retreating Japanese along the coast, some units, principally the bulk of a battalion of the Japanese 238th Regiment, branching out to the jungle, the bulk of survivors passing through Sio. There the 9th was relieved by the 5th militia, the 8th Brigade moving into the forward area. Inland, the enemy exhausted themselves on the jungle track to Tarikgnan, some fifteen miles inland from Saidor, where Major-General Nakai had a covering force – the III/239th Battalion and five companies of the 78th Regiment. The Americans extended their comfortable perimeter to a radius of about five miles at Saidor and waited for the Australians to join them.

The 8th Brigade were nearly all inexperienced, but well trained at the jungle course at Canungra in south Queensland, and there was the usual nervous firing at night. They were supported by an AIF battery of short 25-pounders, AIF and militia engineers, and Papuan riflemen who had fought extremely well with the 9th Division at Finschhafen. Dexter justly includes them in the annals: 'The Papuans were in their element as hunters and were busy looking for scattered bands of Japanese. They would have been disappointed had they been recalled (as was intended at one stage) and, as events turned out two companies of Papuans could probably have advanced to Saidor quicker and with less effort than any brigade of Australians.' They began clearing the way in a spectacular fashion: Corporal Bengari 'whose reputation was similar to that of the best of the Gurkhas' led his section of five men in an ambush on twenty-nine Japanese and killed them all before they could fire one defensive shot. The first day's advance was cleared before the brigade had even started forward.

The natives, who eventually formed five battalions, loved the ritual and drill of army life; they were supremely confident in the jungle and their losses were remarkably light, only eighty-five being killed and 201 wounded during the whole New Guinea campaign; and they were to receive sixty-five decorations for bravery in action and 297 were awarded the Long Service Medallion.

No 4 Squadron, RAAF, examined closely from their Boomerangs and Wirraways every yard of ground ahead, counting corpses, peering into empty villages, checking bridges or lack of them over the many creeks, and reporting 'the expressions on the faces of retreating Japanese'. The only thing that delayed the advance was a breakdown in the supply system; otherwise the enemy kept running, hunted and starved, back towards Saidor. A considerable force was found at Tapen village where the Australians charged with automatics firing while the Papuans came in on a flank; 142 Japanese were killed without loss to the attackers. Corporal Bengari and two of his men killed forty-three. At that village human flesh was found cooking in a pot. Along this coast a small skinny Japanese had given himself up, afraid, he said, of being ordered by his sergeant to report to the kitchen without his dixie. During the chase a relatively large number of Japanese – forty-eight – were taken prisoner, and an extraordinarily large number – 1,793 – were found dead along the tracks, either killed by aircraft strikes, native attacks, illness or starvation. 734 were killed by the brigade. The only casualties suffered by Australians and

Papuans were three killed and five wounded.

The chance for the Americans at Saidor to march into the hills and attack the enemy group there was lost by their inactivity. Blamey wrote to Berryman: 'About 8,000 semi-starved, ill equipped and dispirited Japanese bypassed Saidor. It was disappointing that the fruits of victory were not fully reaped, and that once again the remnants of 51st Division escaped our clutches.' American observers had counted, and not blasted, over 3,000 passing through Tarikgnan. The US 162nd Regiment took over the chase from the Australians and gave their reinforcements experience in traversing mountainous coastlines jagged with ravines.

The objectives now were Bogadjim and Madang, after a meeting could be effected with the 7th Division moving down the winding Japanese road from the Finisterres. They were also widely spread along native tracks, covering an area of about twenty miles in width, and patrols headed inland to approach Madang from the west. Trucks, carts, weapons and ammunition were falling into Australian hands along the Bogadjim road. Enemy patrolling on both flanks was rarely aggressive, usually inquisitive to know from whom he was retreating. On 17th April the 15th Brigade, the militiamen who had been in New Guinea for more than a year, walked into Bogadjim.

Now the 5th Division came back to the scene, moved on to Madang with part of the 11th Division and there, at the large base which had been in Japanese hands for about two years, they caught glimpses of the rearguard of the Japanese Eighteenth Army retreating through Alexishafen towards Wewak. Adachi hoped to get his army to Hollandia, across the border into Dutch New Guinea, before that logically valuable base was invaded by the Allies. Before becoming established at Wewak, he had to get more than 30,000 men across the wide delta and extensive marshes of the Sepik river, handicapped by attacks by aircraft and torpedo boats, clouds of mosquitoes, mud and strong river currents. This delay gave an advantage of time for the Allies to get to Hollandia.

Green Island, north of Bougainville, had already been invaded, on 15th February, by the 3rd New Zealand Division and, on the 29th, US Cavalry landed on Los Negros Island in the Admiralties, a group about 200 miles north of Madang and 300 miles northwest of Rabaul. On 20th March the island of Emirau, east of the Admiralties, was invaded.

The Joint Chiefs of Staff instructed General MacArthur to neutralise Rabaul and Kavieng (New Ireland) and speed the development of an air and naval base at Los Negros and Manus in the Admiralties. Wewak and Hansa Bay were to be by-passed and enemy forces enveloped by seizing Hollandia from where air strikes could be made against the Palaus, western New Guinea and the Halmaheras. Then, from his New Guinea bases and from the large harbour at Manus, army and navy forces could gather for the invasion of the Palaus and Mindanao in the Philippines.

A party of experienced Australians was landed by US submarine to probe the Hollandia area about which little was known; by comparison with Papua-New Guinea, the Dutch territories had hardly been explored by Europeans. The reconnaissance party were betrayed by natives almost as soon as they had landed and, although they inflicted many casualties on the Japanese, most of them were killed or captured. The invasions of Aitape and Hollandia were made by I American Corps (24th and 41st Divisions) commanded by General Eichelberger. Opposition was weak from the predominantly base troops (611 actually surrendered at Hollandia) and within forty-eight hours two wings of RAAF Kittyhawk fighters

American troops storm ashore to take Wakde Island

were landing on Tadji airfield to go dogfighting, strafing or bombing. Eichelberger described Hollandia's future: '. . . one of the great bases of the war. In the deep waters of Humboldt Bay a complete fleet could lie at anchor. Tremendous docks were constructed, and 135 miles of pipeline were led over the hills to feed gasoline to the airfields . . . a city of 140,000 men took occupancy.' Long before that was accomplished, there were the remnants of the Japanese 41st, 20th and 51st fighting infantry divisions cut off and willing, even in their weakened state, to fight anybody. But the New Guinea campaign was virtu-

ally over. All that remained was to contain the enemy and develop new bases on the mainland and on islands that lay in the general direction of the Philippines.

The US 41st Division sailed out from Hollandia and took Wakde Island and its airfield, just off the coast and 120 miles west of Hollandia, and Biak Island, another 130 miles further west.

Wakde was an easy matter, but Biak cost the Americans 400 killed. The Japanese lost 6,000 in that fighting that lasted from 10th April to 22nd July. Heavy attrition in the battle for Biak denied the Japanese use of their land-based planes to support their navy in the Battle of the Philippine Sea, which ended in a spectacular victory for the US Navy.

Containment

Admiral Halsey's drive through the Solomons was a series of taking, or constructing, air bases as each island was occupied. In February 1943 US Army and Marine assault battalions landed unopposed to develop airfields on Pavavu and Banika Islands, about eighty miles from Henderson Field; in July the US 43rd Division landed on New Georgia Island where, by August, the airfields of Segi and Munda were operational; in October, Marines landed on Choiseul and the 8th New Zealand Brigade landed on Treasury Island; and, on 1st November, the 3rd Marine Division of the 1st Marine Amphibious Corps made their main landing on Bougainville. The services of coast watchers were very valuable in these operations. Halsey relied on their reef and tidal measurements – in that area tides were sometimes erratic and unpredictable – on their advice regarding entrances to lagoons and possible landing areas, and on their observations of enemy installations and movements. With knowledge of the enemy's naval code and the services of the coast watchers, Halsey's Intelligence was well equipped for these campaigns.

De-coding Japanese messages en-

abled the USAAF to send out
Lightnings on a successful interception of Yamamoto's transport
aircraft, on 18th April, and he was
killed when it was shot down, a few
days after he had set in motion his
Operation *I Go*. Although it resulted
in the loss of some Allied warships
and transports, that air counter-
offensive flown by 200 fighters and 170
bombers, dive-bombers and torpedo-
bombers, was unsuccessful – the
Japanese lost the bulk of their remaining air force in the SWPA. In
taking the airfields on Bougainville,
the Marines suffered less than 2,000

Opposite: Torokina air strips, one of
the objectives of the Allies on
Bougainville. *Above:* Jungle advance
on the island

casualties. The enemy losses were also
lighter than expected when they were
pushed back inland. In the landing by
the 1st Marines at Cape Gloucester,
New Britain, on Boxing Day, they were
supported by a good quantity of 'the
mostest' – including rockets – and were
helped by the Cavalry making a diversionary attack on Atawe. When the
Marines were pushing towards the
airfield, they were halted by a system

of twelve log-bunkers manned by over 250 Japanese. They were all killed when tanks firing 25mm guns blasted the bunkers to pieces.

Monsoons delayed the development of the Cape Gloucester airfield which was not fully serviceable until February. Before they were relieved by the army's 40th Division, the Marines lost 310 killed and 1,083 wounded, while killing 3,868 Japanese. By the end of March, about one third of New Britain, including the Willaumez Peninsula, was in Allied hands. The enemy lost heavily in the Admiralties when the heavily armed Cavalry – 1st, 7th, 8th and 12th Divisions – landed behind enormous air and naval bombardments, and fired thousands of tons of their own shells, rockets and mortars at the small garrison. There were bunkers which were hit by 500-lb aerial bombs, shells from tanks, mortar bombs, machine-gun fire and flame-throwers; and if there were any enemy alive after that combined assault, they were buried by tidying-up bulldozers. Of the reports that came out of the Admiralties fighting, some were very weird – like the Japanese officer who crept up at night to slay, with a sword, an American officer asleep in his bunk; the Japanese column that sang 'Deep in the Heart of Texas' as they marched into an ambush; and the groups who committed mass suicide with hand-grenades held against their bellies. When the campaign there officially ended on 18th May, the Cavalry casualties were found to be approximately the same as those the Marines had suffered on New Britain, and another 3,280 enemy were dead.

As anticipated by Blamey, Australian forces were requested to take over from Americans in what were primarily areas of Australian interest – Australian New Guinea, New Britain and the Northern Solomons-Green Islands-Emirau Island area which included Bougainville. The take-over was to be completed by November 1944. MacArthur envisaged using only two AIF divisions with his ground forces in the advance on the Philippines, while Blamey expected him to use 6th, 7th and 9th – the three veteran divisions; and Blamey planned to have three militia divisions garrison the Solomons, New Britain and the mainland of New Guinea, holding the enemy behind a strongly patrolled perimeter. However, MacArthur objected to this sane, life-saving plan and insisted that Blamey use four divisions and continue the offensive in by-passed areas. In New Guinea and the outer islands there were estimated to be 75,400 enemy troops; actually there were 30,000 in Bougainville, 93,000 in New Britain and 31,000 in Aitape-Wewak, a total of 154,000. Although Australians, particularly the veteran AIF divisions, would have preferred to have gone conquering into the Philippines or Japan itself, there was a logistical reason against them joining their differently equipped ally who, after two years, was now taking over the major share of the land fighting. So seven brigades took over from the six American divisions.

The Japanese garrisons were virtually POW camps where the prisoners fed themselves; nevertheless they had to be guarded – patrolled and contained – in case they broke out in strength to massacre their warders and destroy aircraft and installations. If they dared to sneak into Allied camps to watch movies from behind trees at open air cinemas – as some actually did – they were expected not to bear arms. The Japanese did not consider themselves to be prisoners of war yet and were prepared to continue the fight to the death. There were some islands where the enemy could be safely left to 'wither on the vine' but wherever he was opposed by Australian forces he was willing to fight.

General Imamura's Eighth Area Army HQ was at Rabaul and, in

Marines with essential supplies land at Cape Gloucester

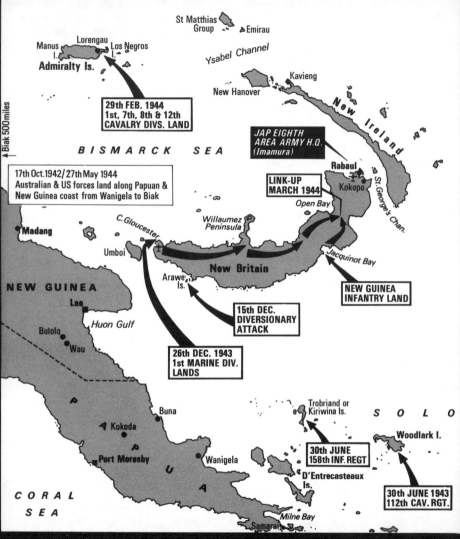

Manus I. Lorengau **Los Negros I.**
Admiralty Is.

St Matthias Group Emirau

Ysabel Channel

Kavieng

New Hanover

New Ireland

← Biak 500 miles

B I S M A R C K   S E A

JAP EIGHTH AREA ARMY H.Q. *(Imamura)*

29th FEB. 1944 1st, 7th, 8th & 12th CAVALRY DIVS. LAND

Rabaul

LINK-UP MARCH 1944

St. George's Chan.

Kokopo

Open Bay

17th Oct.1942/27th May 1944 Australian & US forces land along Papuan & New Guinea coast from Wanigela to Biak

Madang

C. Gloucester

Umboi

Willaumez Peninsula

Jacquinot Bay

New Britain

NEW GUINEA INFANTRY LAND

N E W   G U I N E A

Arawe Is.

15th DEC. DIVERSIONARY ATTACK

Lae

Huon Gulf

Bulolo

Wau

26th DEC. 1943 1st MARINE DIV. LANDS

Buna

P

Kokoda

Trobriand or Kiriwina Is.

S O L O

Woodlark I.

30th JUNE 158th INF. REGT

Port Moresby

Wanigela

U

A

D'Entrecasteaux Is.

30th JUNE 1943 112th CAV. RGT.

C O R A L   S E A

Milne Bay

Samarai

While the Allies were advancing in New Guinea, American and New Zealand forces were island-hopping in the Solomons and Bismark Archipelago

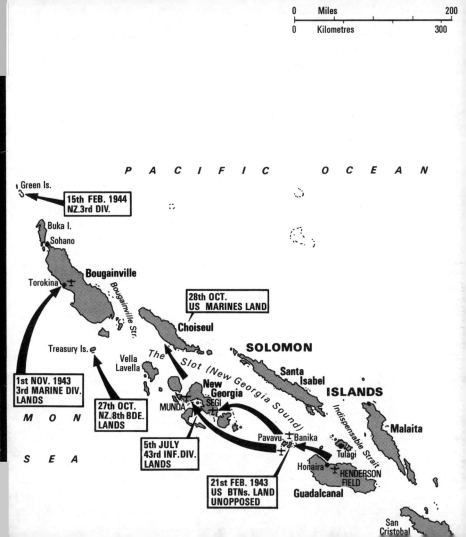

| 0 | Miles | 200 |
| 0 | Kilometres | 300 |

PACIFIC OCEAN

**15th FEB. 1944
NZ.3rd DIV.**

Green Is.

Buka I.
Sohano

Torokina   **Bougainville**

Bougainville Str.

**28th OCT.
US MARINES LAND**

Treasury Is.

Vella
Lavella

The Slot (New Georgia Sound)

Choiseul

SOLOMON

Santa
Isabel

ISLANDS

**1st NOV. 1943
3rd MARINE DIV.
LANDS**

M   O   N

**New
Georgia**

MUNDA   SEGI

**27th OCT.
NZ. 8th BDE.
LANDS**

S   E   A

**5th JULY
43rd INF.DIV.
LANDS**

Pavavu   Banika

**21st FEB. 1943
US BTNs. LAND
UNOPPOSED**

Indispensable Strait

Malaita

Tulagi

Honaira   **HENDERSON
FIELD**

Guadalcanal

San
Cristobal

addition to the 17th and 38th Divisions, he had enough independent brigades and regiments to form another two divisions. On Bougainville he had the 6th Division plus other units. Between Wewak and the Sepik river the Eighteenth Army was still commanded by Adachi who received his orders from Field Marshal Count Terauchi's Southern Army staff.

The airstrip at Torokina was, to the Allies, the only useful piece of territory on the whole of Bougainville. The island's large concentration of enemy troops was too far from New Guinea to be a threat but, because of the airfield, four militia brigades were sent to relieve the Americans – who sold them, through Lease-Lend, an ice cream factory, a soft-drink factory and a cold storage unit. When they left, however, the Americans took most of the transport vessels, and the supply position for the Australians became acute. With a strong air force, which included a RNZAF wing, there was little fear of being raided by enemy aircraft which might have flown from Rabaul or Kavieng, so when the army went on the offensive at the end of December, it had adequate air support.

The first attack was made against the fittest enemy battalion on the island and, although the 25th Battalion employed in this operation had undergone very minor battle experience, they cleared the opposition from a strong defensive position. There weren't many hard little battles like this, and most of the work was patrolling, during which numerous Japanese were killed for very few losses among the militia. A contributing factor to these successes was the textbook, *Tactical and Administrative Doctrine for Jungle Warfare*, written on Bougainville by General Savige, and printed and bound there for distribution to all officers and NCO's. The book provided on-the-spot schooling at a time when it was inconvenient to send men to a specialised training depot.

Opposite and above: The United States 1st Marines land at Cape Gloucester, Bougainville

The enemy resisted Savige's southern drive more strongly but the strain on the Japanese command proved too much for Seventeenth Army's leader, General Hyakutake, who became paralysed on his left side. He had also been worried by criticism from his younger officers regarding his conduct of the campaign. Hyakutake was replaced by Lieutenant-General Kanda, who was, according to the 23rd Brigade historian, a 'shrewd, hard, fussy little professional soldier of long experience. He was steeped in tradition and a ruthless commander, but even his bitterest enemies admitted his capabilities.' Whatever the younger officers planned, they were given no opportunity to experiment and some were relieved of their command. A notable battle was fought at Slater's Knob, on the Puriata river, where some 300 Japanese were killed, many of them in waves of *banzai* attacks that came within a couple of yards of the defenders' weapon pits. Except for several weeks of torrential rain when operations were brought almost to a standstill, action on Bougainville continued until the August ceasefire.

The 8th Battalion fought the last series of actions on the island and, during one of these in which a platoon was held up by fire from camouflaged bunkers, a militiaman, Private F J Partridge, won a Victoria Cross. The young banana grower from Queensland was wounded in the attack but continued to rush forward under heavy fire, picked up a Bren from beside its dead gunner and fired back at Japs in a bunker. As this was ineffective, he went forward with a smoking grenade in one hand, a rifle in the other, threw the grenade through when it was half burnt and when it burst dived into the bunker to kill the last of the surviving Japs. The place where this action took place was then named Part Ridge, the guilty author remaining anonymous.

Brigadier Simpson of the 29th Brigade reported : '. . . I noticed a tendency among all ranks, including officers, to question vigorously the purpose and soundness of operations in the Solomons. It was necessary to bring to the notice of commanders the danger of permitting unchallenged discussion on such a contentious subject. A certain amount of tactful propaganda was necessary to combat the forceful but often misinformed arguments of certain individuals.' The troops were receiving letters from home informing them of the increasing public criticism of the policy of large-scale offensives against the enemy in what should have been by-passed SWPA battlefields. The morale of the troops, however, remained high, as Brigadier Hammer later wrote: '. . . could not have been better if it (the brigade) had been fighting the Alamein battle or capturing Tokyo. Yet every man knew, as well as I knew, that the operations were mopping up and that they were *not* vital to the winning of the war. So they ignored the Australian papers, their relatives' letters advising caution, and got on with the job in hand, fighting and dying as if it was the battle for final victory.'

That 'mopping up' in a senseless campaign cost Australia 516 killed and 1,572 wounded. 8,500 Japanese were killed by Australians and natives, 9,500 died of illness. Some 20,000 had been killed previously by Americans before they handed over during the tacit truce which existed until the Australians went on the offensive.

Before the US 40th Division handed over their patrolling of New Britain to the 5th Australian, in August 1944, a truce also existed on that island where the American air bases were guarded and the main Japanese forces were withdrawn to remote areas. Australian-led natives did most of the patrolling in between the Americans and the Japanese 17th and 32nd Divisions, detachments from several other brigades, 22,000 base and 1 of c (lines of communication) troops and 2,500 naval men. The naval base at Rabaul now only served occasional submarines making nocturnal visits and barges which survived the constant patrolling of Beaufighters, Lightnings and Kittyhawks (Warhawks).

'Cloak and dagger' Melanesian guerillas knocked out enemy coast watchers when the Australians moved in with their militia division. A battalion group and a company of New Guinea infantrymen landed safely at Jacquinot Bay. Advances were made along both sides of the island to Open Bay and Henry Reid Bay – where the island was narrowest – and, in March 1945, joined up, completely cutting off the rest of the island from Rabaul. During this pincer movement, Corporal W C Martin, an AIF member of the 14/32nd Battalion, was leading his section in a position which came under intense mortar fire. When his section was halted on a steep spur near Bacon Hill, by fire from three posts he stood up and shouted, 'They can't do that to me !' Leaving his men behind, he rushed forward alone, firing his Owen gun and throwing grenades, forced the enemy out of the three posts, killed five and fell himself, wounded. The ex-textile operator from Victoria survived to wear his Military Medal.

Many of the New Guinea Battalion were becoming restive; they had been on operations for over seven months and some were anxious to be out of New Britain and back in the fighting on 'the mainland' where the enemy still occupied some of their land. The type of holding action on New Britain annoyed them, especially when they would make a successful patrol, sometimes suffering casualties, to pinpoint an enemy position which was then not attacked by the Australians. Difference in pay between white and black soldiers was also a grievance and their pay was increased from ten shillings to fifteen shillings a month.

For about ten weeks there were constant patrols on the move – officially described as uneventful. In case their morale and fighting efficiency declined, the GOC suggested that the division could undertake 'minor offensive operations against enemy parties' – a breath of life for a general but unnecessary risk to men who knew that it would not be long before 'Japan man 'e cry enough.' Blamey did not approve of any offensive and the position remained static. The relatively inexperienced militiamen (actually a militia division but many of its members had transferred to the AIF) lost fifty-three killed and 140 wounded while containing a Japanese army of 53,000 and more than 16,000 naval men, many of whom were fighting-fit veterans. Obviously General Imamura could have 'banzaied' the Australians into the sea, but his groups would still be stranded on New Britain and a strong retaliatory force would have wiped out every son of Nippon. Perhaps he was waiting for a miracle.

The 35,000 strong remnant of Lieutenant-General Adachi's army at Wewak could field a fighting group the size of about one reinforced brigade group when, in October 1944, the AIF 6th Division, now commanded by Major-General J E S Stevens, took over the garrison at Aitape. The task of the division was to guard the airfield and radar stations, to assist Angau and Allied Intelligence Bureau (AIB) patrols, and to prevent enemy movement westwards. The enemy was spreading rapidly into the fertile and thickly populated country south of the Torricelli mountains where he raided native gardens. Occasional aircraft and submarines brought in medical and ordinance supplies to the coast. The 6th Division were asked to take the coastline to cut off all supplies and isolate the enemy inland and, at the same time, march inland to drive him from the garden area south of the Torricellis. Naturally, he was expected to fight against these strangling advances. Blamey believed that for troops 'to remain inactive for months while awaiting the development of full scale naval and air support is a negation of all military teaching and common sense. It reduces the morale of the troops and leads to disciplinary troubles as seen during the long stay of our troops on the mainland . . . a colossal waste of manpower, material and money . . . reduces rapidly the resistance to tropical diseases and wastage of men increases rapidly . . . encourages the enemy and gives him increasing influence and control over the natives.'

The patrols doggedly hunted the enemy in the mountains and along the coast, some Indian POW'S were rescued; Japanese were killed by the score while Australians were killed in ones and twos. Unusually severe floods drowned men on both sides when the rains poured down in January. Clearing the native gardens of the Japanese pestilence was a dangerous occupation in the blind jungle country where it was still risky for scouts. On one occasion, the enemy made a *banzai* charge on one of their posts which had been captured by men of the 2/2nd Battalion, but they had left it and the enemy charged into an empty hole. During February, the 16th Brigade moved slowly forward on this wasteful drive through the ridges and valleys and along the coast. The natives had seen enough of the evils of Japanese occupation to welcome back the Australians, and those employed as 'sentries' – natives sent back to their own villages to spy and, if possible, kill – accounted for many of the enemy. Sentries tied a knot in a piece of twine to record a kill, knots were tied for enemy numbers observed, and other knots were tied to remind him to report other things seen. Life for the enemy was becoming intolerable, as a Japanese general recorded after the war:

'Once the natives knew where we were they induced aircraft to strafe and bomb us. In addition the natives in the rear rebelled and losses were caused among those of our men who were employed on liaison or food gathering. On top of this at the time rain was falling continuously and the rivers were flooding and the roads were becoming muddy . . . there were attempts at escape by the natives who did not like their task of carrying supplies, and crimes such as the killing of small garrisons. Really, after April, 1945, the state of public order on the western front was very disturbed!' Some natives attached themselves unofficially to patrols just for the enjoyment of the 'hunt'. One of the soldiers wrote: 'They seemed to sense a kill, and often, when a patrol was about to get into a blue, they would appear from nowhere, furtively, silently, like bludgers coming in for mess. They would come with long, murderous spears, with tomahawks and machetes, as keen as boxing fans to see the blood flow, and as disappointed if it didn't.' Note: 'blue' and 'bludger' are Australianese for 'fight' and 'parasite'.

Occasionally, Australian patrols were surrounded, like a troop from the 2/10th Commando Squadron besieged for five days and four nights, surviving intact and killing at least forty-five Japs in the process. Adachi seemed to be going out of his mind at this stage – he thought that there must be several divisions operating against him, whereas it was, at the most, one brigade and a commando squadron. On 18th March he wrote: 'It is not an impossibility for us, using our original all-out fighting tactics, to annihilate the 50,000 or 60,000 enemy troops with our present fighting power . . . leaving thus an impressive record . . . in the annals of our Army and paying a tribute to the Emperor and to the spirits of our numerous fellow dead.' That was a

way of increasing the numbers of his fellow dead. If the order for a Big Banzai had come from Tojo, no doubt there would have been enormous slaughter on both sides in the Aitape area.

The remnants of the Eighteenth army were driven back from the coast and Wewak by the end of May, and were enclosed in the mountains. On the other side of Wewak and the other side of the Sepik, militiamen of the 8th Brigade mopped their way up from Bogadjim at light cost to themselves. Pressure on the enemy was maintained on all sides, so that if Adachi had decided to organise his Big Banzai, his intentions would have been observed in the many signs of war. Eventually, the Eighteenth Army was pushed back to a last-stand area with a radius of about eight miles, some ten miles inland from Wewak; the stand was expected to last until about September and when Field Marshal Terauchi was advised of the plan he honoured the army with a citation. Adachi made up his mind 'not to set foot on my country's soil again but to remain as a clod of earth in the Southern Seas with the 100,000 officers and men . . .' But he eventually thought better of it and surrendered with his remaining 13,500 troops.

During June, an American Cub pilot, Lieutenant Barnes, picked up a message, suspended between two poles, from a subadar-major and twenty-eight other members of the 1/14th Punjab Regiment, prisoners of war from Singapore who had been brought down as labourers to New Guinea by their captors. Food, clothing and arms were dropped to them and eventually, when they were brought out, they described how hundreds of Japanese had died moving from Hansa Bay to the Sepik.

The 6th Division, which had suffered more than 4,000 casualties in Libya, Greece and Crete, lost 442 killed and 1,141 wounded in this, their last, campaign; another 128 died from tropical diseases and accidents and

Attacking the Japanese coastal shipping route in Hansa Bay

16,203 were admitted to hospital, some of them more than once, many for only a few days, with malaria, skin diseases, dysentery, dengue, scrub typhus and other environmental complaints. While clearing the enemy from some 3,000 square miles they killed 9,000 and took 269 prisoners.

There were over 2,000 Japanese prisoners of war in Australia by August, 1944. They were well fed and healthy, but they considered that the humane treatment they received was a subversive way of placating them, that the Australians were therefore morally and spiritually weak, and were secretly afraid of the prisoners. On the night of 7th-8th August, a Japanese bugle sounded in a POW camp, near the western New South Wales town of Cowra, and the prisoners made a banzai charge, armed with knives, baseball bats, clubs studded with nails and hooks, wire stilettoes and garotting cords. About 400 broke through the wire by throwing blankets over it and flinging themselves across. Two guards punched their way through the mass of Japanese, manned a Vickers machine-gun and fired it until they were knifed and clubbed to death. The gun jammed when the Japs swung it around onto the guards' huts and those would-be gunners were shot. Some set fire to the huts while about 200 crouched in a ditch which was swept by machine-gun and rifle

bullets until dawn. Then they surrendered. Hundreds of prisoners escaped to the country where guards, men from a training unit nearby, and two policemen rounded them up over a period of several days. A third guard had been killed and three were wounded; 234 Japanese died – from bullets, in the burning huts or by hanging themselves from trees in the countryside, and 108 were wounded.

When they met at Honolulu in July, 1944, President Roosevelt approved MacArthur's grand plan for the encroachment on Japan. Nevertheless, the Joint Chiefs of Staff argued for three months on the question whether to take Yap, Talaud and Mindanao on the way to Leyte and Luzon, or to let Admiral King have his way and throw everything into a full-scale descent on Formosa and establish a bridgehead on the China coast at Amoy. The Joint Chiefs were inclined to think that the Philippines would be the quicker route to Japan and were convinced when, in September, Admiral Halsey struck the Philippines with his carriers against surprisingly weak resistance. Halsey suggested that the Yap, Talaud and Mindanao plans be scrapped in favour of an early direct landing on Leyte Gulf. The logistics planning for this operation began when the Joint Chiefs gave the go-ahead signal in October.

Nimitz offered his amphibious force intended for Yap to MacArthur. The offer was accepted by Sutherland who was acting in MacArthur's absence – although Sutherland knew that enemy strength on Leyte was greater than Halsey thought. The Intelligence Officer was as keen as MacArthur to return to the Philippines. Luzon was invaded on 20th December and, in the Central Pacific, Iwo Jima, the Bonins and Okinawa were invaded between January and March, 1945.

The last Australian campaign was fought on Borneo, an island large enough to encompass all the Philippine islands, and its small neighbour, Tarakan. This was a wasteful operation which began after Germany had been defeated and Americans were already established on Okinawa. There were serious manpower shortages in Australia, and Blamey suggested reducing the front line divisions. The acting Prime Minister, Mr Ben Chifley, who had taken over on the death of Mr Curtin, recommended to MacArthur that the 7th Division should not be committed to Borneo and that only the 9th should be sent. Of course, there should not have been any new campaigns in the SWPA and, whether MacArthur thought this or not, he followed his orders, as he explained in his reply to Chifley: 'The Borneo campaign . . . has been ordered by the Joint Chiefs of Staff who are charged by the Combined Chiefs of Staff with the responsibility for strategy in the Pacific . . . not now possible to substitute another division . . . no specific plans as far as I know for employment of Australian troops after the Borneo Campaign . . .'

The campaign was futile and should never have been ordered. Biak had been expensive but strategically useful. On Borneo the troops felt they were in a useless backwater and Lieutenant-Colonel Byrne's report on his battalion's 'mopping up' operations on Bougainville also applied here: 'I think that collectively the officers and men of the battalion did a grand job. It was filthy country; they were fighting what seemed to be a useless campaign and they knew it. Men are not fools and even though each man realised he was fighting for something which could benefit his country very little (and in addition his fighting received very little credit or publicity) he carried out orders energetically and in a very fine spirit.'

The reason why Australian troops were sent to Borneo was mysteriously political, probably prompted by Britain or America. Militarily, it was an illogical move and Gavin Long places the decision on the home government: 'For part of the last year of the war the Australian Army in the field was larger in proportion to population than that of any of the Allies, except perhaps Russia. The Government's motives in maintaining the national effort at so high a level appear to have been a wish that Australia should pull her full weight, and an ambition to gain international esteem and a position of influence in the peace. It is an illusion to which small nations are prone that the policy of foreign allies, as distinct from those with whom patriotic sentiments are shared, are influenced by such emotions as gratitude for past support.'

So the 7th and 9th went in to Tarakan, Labuan, Brunei and Balikpapan, knocking out strongpoints, holding perimeters, releasing Indian prisoners and meeting head-hunting Dyaks who sought payment for fresh Japanese heads. The campaign began on 1st May and the last battle was fought not long before the first atomic bomb was dropped on Japan. They lost 568 killed and 1,534 were wounded in operations which won back a derelict oilfield and killed some 5,000 of the enemy.

'In the Jacquinot Bay area the darkness was broken by coloured flares fired from ships in port; machine-guns rattled; tracers streaked up into the heavens. There was singing and shouting and long blasts from motor horns . . . In the hospital wards sisters and orderlies sang with the patients. By now several fires

New Guinea surrender. Adachi arrives at Wewak to hand over his sword

were visible as merry-makers ignited some disused buildings in old camp sites. This joyous scene continued until almost morning.' Historians were everyone recording reaciton to the Japanese surrender. Native runners were sent to coastal and hill villages to spread the good news. Many Japanese believed the surrender was merely a temporary measure but the bulk of them in New Guinea had

been convinced that surrender was inevitable. At Wewak, on 13th September, Major-General H C H Robertson, COC of the 6th Division, received surrender from Lieutenant-General Adachi. In 1947, Adachi was sentenced to life imprisonment for his war crimes which included condoning the

Above: Lieutenant-General Kanda and Lieutenant-General Savige negotiate the surrender of Bourgainville. *Below:* The final act; Kanda hands over his sword

killing of prisoners of war. At Bougainville, on 8th September, Major-General Savige received the surrender of Major-General Kanda and his 23,570 officers and men, all that remained of the force of 65,000 on the island when American troops landed in November 1943.

The natives of New Guinea went back to their settled life as gardeners, fishermen, itinerant labourers and servants. The war had made an enormous impact on their lives and remote villages had been visited by white men for the first time. What had impressed them most was the amount of goods that the Allies could call up from Australia where an all-powerful white god taught them the secret techniques of manufacture. In the Madang area this fetish for European goods became part of a new social system inspired by an ex-police boy, Yali. He had been acclaimed for heroic deeds performed while a member of a coast watching unit in Dutch New Guinea, and after the war he was taken on a tour of some Queensland towns by Angau officials. He returned to the Madang district where he introduced his new system, based on a 'cargo cult'. Its object was to secure for its devotees, by sympathetic magic, the material blessings they had acquired a taste for during the battle for the island. It was quasi-military in that village huts were aligned in rows, the paths between kept clean, whistles blew for getting up and for beginning breakfast, women were to be free to all men as they were in soldiers' brothels and, because he thought tables with bowls of flowers in Queensland houses were set there to invoke the gods, Yali advised villagers to place cloths over tables and gather flowers for bowls. In June 1947, Yali went to Moresby to collect the hoped for trucks, machinery, electric light plant, tools and other goods while his followers maintained look-outs along the coast for the cargo ships. Some villagers cleared strips in the jungle and formed poles and branches in the shape of aeroplanes to entice cargo-laden Dakotas down to earth. Because too many people were refusing to work, waiting for the cargoes which never came, Yali was arrested and sentenced to a few years in prison; when he was released he gave up his cargo cult, threw away his neatly pressed shorts and vest, and returned to more rational, time-tested tribal customs. Even now there are scattered examples of cargo cults surviving in the south-west Pacific.

In a letter General MacArthur sent to Prime Minister Curtin, in 1944, he wrote lengthily on the future of New Guinea and South-East Asia. These are some of his views expressed in that letter:

'It may be assumed that there will be other Pacific conflicts in the next half century, for the reason that the fundamental interests of the UK, US, USSR, China, Japan, and other nations, in relation to the control of axial centres and undeveloped economic areas, still require adjustment, and doubtless will provoke forceful measures to that end.

'Such adjustments may or may not be carried out through formal processes of war, although they are likely to be; but at least they will lead to conflicts in which the outcome will be governed largely by constant strategic factors.

'Australia will have learned nothing from the sacrifice of this war if the world strategic importance of the whole New Guinea theatre has not become overwhelmingly obvious to the nation.'

Of New Guinea's future, Blamey also had very strong feelings, as John Hetherington explains in his biography of the late Field Marshal: 'Blamey's vision of Australia's place in the Pacific was at the root of his incessant preaching that New Guinea must be developed. He saw it as the Australian mainland's shield against attack from the north in any Pacific conflict.'

Bibliography

Jungle Road to Tokyo by R L Eichelberger (Viking Press, New York)
General Kenny Reports by George C Kenny (Duell, New York)
MacArthur 1941-1951: *Victory in the Pacific* by C A Willoughby and J Chamberlain (Heinemann, London)
Retreat from Kokoda by Raymond Paull (Heinemann, London)
The War with Japan by Charles Bateson (Barrie & Rockliff, London. Michigan State University Press, Michigan)
If I Die by Malcolm Wright (Landsdowne Press, London)
The Coast Watchers by Eric Feldt (Pacific Books, London. Tri-Ocean, San Francisco)
Hunted by M Murray (Angus & Robertson, London. Tri-Ocean, San Francisco)
A Short History of New Guinea by Biskup, Jinks and Nelson (Angus & Robertson, London
The Challenge of New Guinea by Grenfell Price (Angus & Robertson, London)
The Brave Japanese by Kenneth Harrison (Angus & Robertson, London. Tri-Ocean, San Francisco)